Before You Leap

Before You Leap

Leap

**What a Lawyer Wants You
to Know About Starting
a Gig Economy Business**

Joel Ankney, Esq.

ISBN 13: 9781686557071
Library of Congress Control Number: 2019912577
Independently Published using Amazon
Kindle Direct Publishing Platform
Virginia Beach, Virginia

This book is for my kids because they might need it sometime in their careers.

I hope it helps.

TABLE OF CONTENTS

ACKNOWLEDGMENTS

Thanks to Jenny for her encouragement and input.

Thanks to everyone who read my first book. You gave me the courage to write another.

Thanks to Amtrak for great service. About 95% of this book was written while traveling by train.

Thanks to Shay for expert editing.

Thanks to my gig economy clients for entrusting me with their startups, contracts, and disputes.

ABOUT THE AUTHOR

THERE ARE ABOUT ONE MILLION lawyers in the United States. Some probably have helped clients start a gig economy business. What makes me one in a million? It's the combination of academics and experience.

I graduated first in my class from William & Mary Law School. I also earned a bachelor's degree in psychology from Brigham Young University.

I have been practicing law for 28 years. I have worked at some of the largest law firms in the USA and as a solo practitioner. I've helped a lot of people handle the legal issues associated with starting and running a gig economy business in a variety of industries. I probably haven't seen it all, but I've seen most of it. I can smoothly guide my clients through the business startup process because I have helped them down that road many times before. I know what to look for, what questions to ask, what to expect, what's customary, and what's reasonable.

This unique combination of academics and experience provides my clients with legal representation that helps reduce their risks when starting and running a gig economy business.

I AM NOT YOUR LAWYER BECAUSE YOU READ THIS BOOK

WE NEED TO TAKE CARE of some business before we start. What I am about to write might sound a bit harsh, but it helps me sleep better. Lawyers call this a "Disclaimer."

Writing a book creates a risk for a lawyer, so I want to clear up our relationship from the beginning. Our relationship is only author-reader; it is not lawyer-client.

A client can sue a lawyer for bad legal advice. Books by lawyers can create the impression that the reader is the author's client and that the author is giving the reader legal advice.

This book is only for informational purposes. It is designed to help you understand the legal aspects of starting and running a gig economy business. It is not a substitute for legal advice.

Although I am a lawyer, I am not your lawyer. Reading this book does not make me your lawyer, and it doesn't make you my client. If you want me to become your lawyer, we can talk, and, if we are both in agreement, go through the process of making that happen.

Also, I am licensed to practice law only in Virginia. The information in this book is based on my experiences practicing law in Virginia. You might live in another state or country. The laws of your state or country might be different from Virginia's laws. If you want to know what the laws of your state or country are, you need to speak with a lawyer licensed in your state or country.

This book contains stories to illustrate principles. All the examples are based on true stories, although I have combined experiences or altered them to better illustrate concepts and to protect identities. I also don't use anyone's real name.

This book is not considered legal advice; it contains information about legal topics. You use the information in this book at your own risk.

If you want legal advice, you should hire a lawyer. I strongly encourage you to do so. See Chapter Five for guidance.

I'm available. You can find me at joelankney.com.

INTRODUCTION

LOOK BEFORE YOU LEAP.

I grew up in Rockville, Maryland, just a short drive from the Potomac River. My friends and I spent a lot of time in and around the water. When I was a teenager, we started jumping off a low bridge into Seneca Creek where the C&O Canal crosses it at Riley's Lock. The drop was about 15 feet.

Then we heard about a cliff on the Maryland side of Great Falls where generations of high school students had jumped into the Potomac. We got some general directions about where to find it. On a summer afternoon, a few of us hiked down the C&O Canal towpath until we found a trail into the woods that lead to the cliff.

The cliff was terrifying. It was about 60 feet above the river. There was a flat rock at the top of the cliff that gave a jumper about 15 feet of space to run up to the edge for the jump. The granite cliff gradually jutted out into the river as it got closer to the water. The water was rapid and turbulent, making it impossible to see what was under its surface.

There were already a few people at the cliff when we arrived. We watched as they launched themselves over it into the river. We watched the route they took to climb back up the cliff to jump again. We asked questions about the water, where to jump, and whether there were any underwater obstacles to avoid. We asked how far out you had to launch yourself to clear the bottom of the cliff. We wanted to know everything we could about the risks of jumping. Eventually, all of us took turns making multiple jumps off the cliff without incident.

Let me pause here to tell you a few things. I don't endorse or encourage jumping off cliffs, especially at Great Falls. What we did was very dangerous and illegal. In fact, the day after our initial visit to the cliff, my friends returned without me to introduce some others to the cliff (I didn't go because I stayed home to mow the lawn before my parents returned from work). I recall the National Park Service cited them for breaking the law. In addition, I remember hearing stories about other kids in my high school who injured themselves or got caught up in the river and narrowly escaped tragedy. Just writing those few paragraphs above brought back memories that made me shiver as I once again realized how stupid and lucky we were.

Starting a gig economy business is like jumping off a cliff into a river or lake. You want to know the risks before doing so. Learning about the risks will help you determine how to abate or avoid them. There are plenty of books that can help you with the business-related risks of starting a gig economy business. This book identifies and suggests ways to handle the most common legal risks.

A gig economy business is a business that consists of finding and engaging in "gigs" to make money. A gig is a project, usually to provide services to a client. A gig economy business makes money on a project-by-project, contract basis. Gig economy businesses are often labeled as independent contractors, consultants, or freelancers. They are not usually started to obtain investment money, to set the business up for a public offering, or to sell the business (except when the owners are ready to exit the business, such as for retirement). Gig economy businesses are nimble and lean. Many have only one or two owners. They may work from home, other remote locations, leased workspaces, or their client's offices.

You might start a gig economy business at some time in your life. If you work as an employee in the service industry, you might open your own business to provide those services. Or, you might decide to strike out on your own by opening a service business, even if you don't have any experience.

I have been helping people start and run gig economy businesses since before that term was coined. Gig economy businesses I have represented include:
- Software developers
- Website developers
- Cybersecurity consultants

- IT consultants
- Architecture consultants
- Data analytics consultants
- Defense consultants
- Military and law enforcement consultants
- Firefighter consultants
- Healthcare practice management consultants
- Marketing and advertising experts
- Subject matter experts
- Personal fitness trainers and instructors
- Graphic artists
- Commercial photographers
- Commercial videographers
- Physicians
- Lawyers
- Engineers
- Pool service company
- Custom cabinet maker
- Kitchen and bath cabinet installer
- Construction subcontractors
- Auto mechanics
- Handymen

My years of experience helping these clients have provided me with many opportunities to identify and resolve the legal risks associated with starting and running a gig economy business. This book is designed to share those experiences and insights with you. It will help you identify and decide how to reduce or eliminate those risks. Hopefully, following the guidance in this book will help your business run smoothly and help you sleep better.

This book is organized to follow the first steps in the life cycle of a startup gig economy business.

Chapter One is about the legal issues related to choosing and starting an entity.

Your services will create valuable output—work product—that might be protected by copyright, trademark, or trade secret law. Protecting and exploiting intellectual property rights can be some of the stickiest and riskiest issues when starting a gig economy business. Chapter Two discusses intellectual property: how to identify it, protect it, and exploit it.

Chapter Three talks about how to use contracts with clients.

Chapter Four suggests approaches to resolving legal disputes with clients.

Chapter Five helps you decide whether you need outside help with your legal issues, and, if so, how to find it.

Finally, Chapter Six contains checklists to summarize the information in this book and to suggest next steps to help you get started.

This book is your "coach-in-a-box" for starting your gig economy business. Keep this book close and refer to it as a starting point to identify and determine how to handle legal issues. This book is not a substitute for a lawyer, but it can help guide you. It can set expectations about legal risks. It also can help you work more efficiently with any lawyer you engage, which should result in a better client-lawyer relationship, resulting in lower legal fees and better legal services.

This book helps you look before you leap.

1

STARTING A GIG ECONOMY BUSINESS

PATTI WAS A PARTNER AT a large consulting firm where she advised clients on information technology matters. One of her friends became the Chief Information Officer of a large corporation. Patti's friend encouraged her to start her own IT consulting business to become a consultant to his corporation and other businesses on a project-by-project, contract basis.

Patti engaged me because she wanted help choosing the type of legal entity to use for her new business and to create a template contract she could use with her clients. I also recommended she allow me to review her current employment agreement to determine whether it might contain any restrictions on Patti's ability to start and run her gig economy business. My objectives when advising Patti were to protect her personal assets and to see that the relationships with her clients were set up in a way to protect her business interests and help her make a good living.

YOUR GIG ECONOMY BUSINESS COMES WITH RISK.

Starting and running a gig economy business triggers several legal risks.

You risk having a former employer claim you have taken something it owns (like clients, ideas, trade secrets, or copyrighted materials) to run your business.

You risk exposing your personal assets to claims of business creditors. For example, if you run your gig economy business as a sole proprietorship and a disgruntled client sues you and wins, that client could get to your personal bank account to satisfy the judgment.

You risk disagreements with your clients about whether you have adequately performed or delivered. Have you made legally binding promises about your services or deliverables? Even if you haven't, does the law imply certain promises on you?

You risk having a client claim it owns work product, know-how, or expertise. What does the client think it is paying for? What do you think the client is paying for? Many times, the answers to these questions are dramatically different.

You risk subcontractors failing to perform.

You risk not getting paid by a client.

You also risk missing many legal details if you don't get a lawyer to help with these issues.

You can reduce or eliminate these risks by the way you set up and run your gig economy business.

ARE YOU RESTRICTED FROM OPENING YOUR GIG ECONOMY BUSINESS?

Roger was a junior executive at a large corporation, seemingly with lots of promise for fast promotion into upper management. He had made a name for himself inside the company by using software to analyze the company's data to find more opportunities to make money. He even won company awards for his work.

The company merged into a larger competitor that had its own management team. Roger was not part of the new team and could see the writing on the wall. He decided to open his own gig economy business to use his expertise, know-how, and software experience to help other companies analyze data to increase revenue.

Roger had an employment agreement that contained provisions about confidentiality and the ownership of his ideas, concepts, and work product. He wondered whether anything in his contract might prevent him from opening his business.

Like Roger, you may have a great idea for a gig economy business. Where did that idea come from? Is it related to your current employment? If so, do you have a written employment agreement with your current employer? Or, have you signed any type of contract with your employer, such as a confidentiality agreement or an intellectual property ownership agreement? Even if you don't have a contract with your employer, does your employer have an employee handbook or employment policies? Even if your answer is "no" to these questions, are you breaching any federal or state laws your current employer might be able to enforce against you if you start your gig economy business?

Many employers are savvy about the value of their employees' expertise and know-how, and the work product they create. They also understand the worth of their confidential information, such as client lists, client preferences, client contacts, vendor and supplier information, pricing methodology, internal financial information, research and development efforts and results, and business methods and techniques. Some of that confidential information might be valuable simply because it's kept secret, like a secret recipe, secret software code, or a secret algorithm. As a result, employers might require employees to sign contracts to protect that information. Those contracts might range from a comprehensive employment agreement that contains restrictive provisions to narrow-purpose contracts that restrict certain types of activities.

An employer's contract might contain provisions about who owns the ideas, concepts, secrets, and work product an employee develops or creates as part of her employment.

An employer might have an employee handbook or written policies that cover those same issues. Even if you didn't sign a written contract with your employer, you might have signed a legal document indicating your receipt of (and even review and agreement to) an employee handbook or written employment policies.

The law might contain restrictions or address ownership issues, even when you don't have an employment agreement, an employee handbook, or employee policies. For example, the trade secrets statute for the state in which you work will define what a trade secret is and prohibit its misappropriation. And, the US Copyright Act indicates that an employer owns the copyrights to work product created by an employee within the scope of her employment.

You need to research whether any of these sources (contracts, handbooks, policies, and laws) might create a risk that would prevent you from starting and running your gig economy business. If you have a contract, handbook, or employee policy that includes provisions about confidentiality, non-solicitation, non-competition, or ownership of intellectual property rights (e.g., ideas, concepts, copyrights, trade secrets, trademarks, or patents), have a lawyer who has experience with those issues review and advise you on their impact before you move forward.

Even if a contract, handbook, or policy might appear to restrict or prevent you from starting and running your business, your lawyer can advise you on their enforceability. This analysis won't reduce your risk, but it will help you quantify it. You might be able to move forward regardless of the restrictions if your lawyer believes they are unenforceable and you are willing to risk the time and effort of a fight and potential loss if your employer decides to try to enforce the restrictions. Roger decided to take the risk. My analysis of his employment agreement gave him confidence that, if challenged, the contractual provisions of concern could not be enforced.

Consult with a lawyer about how applicable laws might restrict or prohibit your new business. Tell the lawyer what you plan to do, how you plan to do it, what you will use to do it, and the origin of your ideas and methods. Then the lawyer can analyze your proposed gig economy business in light of those applicable laws.

Don't think you can avoid these issues because your employer will never find out; employers always seem to find out. I had a client in Virginia who took a risk based on his prediction that a California company wouldn't find out about his work. Shortly after my client launched his business, an executive from the California company was at a cocktail party in San Francisco and met someone from Virginia. After introductions, the person from Virginia asked the California executive whether he had heard about my client. He hadn't, but after he did, he reported to the company's lawyer, resulting in a letter to my client demanding it stop operating its business in a manner that infringed upon the California company's rights.

Do your legal due diligence before you launch your gig economy business. Get as much comfort as you can from your lawyer that what you intend to do is not restricted or prohibited. Doing this research at the beginning will avoid a lot of problems. Even if you get the news that you shouldn't launch your business, that's valuable information.

USE A LEGAL ENTITY TO PROTECT YOUR PERSONAL ASSETS.

You will get a lot of unsolicited advice about using a legal entity when you tell people you are thinking about starting a gig economy business. Friends, family, colleagues, and even strangers will tell you about C corporations (so-called because they are taxed under Subchapter C of the Internal Revenue Code), S corporations (so-called because they are taxed under Subchapter S of the Internal Revenue Code), and limited liability companies (LLCs). You may also hear about sole proprietorships and partnerships.

The key reason for using a legal entity is to create a barrier between your personal assets and your business liabilities. You don't want to put your personal assets at risk by leaving them unprotected and available to satisfy a business liability, like a client's lawsuit for a refund of money. C Corporations, S Corporations, and LLCs create that barrier; sole proprietorships and partnerships do not.

Of course, many business creditors, such as lenders, credit card companies, and landlords, are aware of the protections a legal entity provides, and require personal guarantees from the business owner. A personal guaranty is a contract that allows the creditor to ignore that barrier of protection and get to your personal assets to satisfy a business liability, such as rent or unpaid bills. The fact that some creditors can get around that barrier, however, does not mean the legal entity is pointless or of no value. There will be other instances where personal guarantees are not required, such as in your contracts with clients, where the barrier created by your legal entity can eliminate the risk to your personal assets.

USE A LIMITED LIABILITY COMPANY (LLC) FOR YOUR GIG ECONOMY BUSINESS, UNLESS YOU HAVE A GOOD REASON NOT TO.

So which type of legal entity should you choose for your gig economy business? Lawyers and accountants offer presentations, classes, and sometimes even free consultations about the differences between legal entities. This topic often is referred to by them as "Choice of Entity." You also can find a huge amount of information on this topic with a simple internet search.

Choice of entity can seem very confusing, but it's not for a gig economy business.

Consider the following factors when choosing which type of legal entity to use:

- Does the entity create the liability barrier explained above?
- Is the entity taxed in a way that benefits you?
- How easy is the entity to manage from a legal perspective?
- What other benefits might the entity offer you?

- Do your circumstances dictate you use a particular type of legal entity?

Don't use a sole proprietorship because it doesn't create the liability barrier you want. If you are the only owner of a business and you don't create a legal entity, you are automatically a sole proprietorship. That's bad because your personal assets—savings accounts, car, home, boat, etc.—are now fully at risk to satisfy business liabilities.

Don't use a partnership either because it also doesn't create the liability barrier you want. If there are two or more owners of the business, and you don't create a legal entity, you are automatically a partnership. Being in a partnership is even worse than running a sole proprietorship. Each partner has the right to legally bind the whole partnership without the agreement of the other partners. And each partner's personal assets are at risk for 100% of any partnership liability, regardless of the partner's percentage of ownership in the partnership. If you have the deepest pocket of all the partners, you will be taking on the most risk in a partnership.

Now that we have quickly narrowed your choices down to a C corporation, an S corporation, and an LLC, let's get rid of one more.

A C corporation creates the liability barrier you want, so that's a good start, but the way it is taxed is not attractive to most gig economy business owners. A C corporation has two tiers of taxation. First, the C corporation is taxed on its net revenues. Second, the shareholders are taxed on any money the corporation distributes to them. Other legal entities don't have two tiers of taxation, so they are more attractive to a gig economy business founder.

In addition, a C corporation requires you to follow a lot of corporate formalities that don't match the nimbleness most gig economy businesses seek. For example, the corporation needs a board of directors and corporate officers. Corporate decisions must be approved by the directors and, sometimes, even the shareholders, in formal meetings or written consents.

So, don't use a C corporation, unless you have a good reason to do so (see below).

Now we've narrowed it down to two legal entities that typically are the best choices for a gig economy business: the S corporation and the LLC. In the 28 years I have been practicing law, there seems to have been (and still is) a lot of debate about which is better. Most of that debate appears to apply to businesses launched with the hope of obtaining investment money and growing significantly. Most gig economy businesses aren't concerned with those objectives, however, which makes the choice of entity easier.

The S corporation satisfies two of the significant criteria: (1) it creates a liability barrier to protect personal assets, and (2) it is a "pass-through" entity for tax purposes. A pass-through entity is a legal entity that is taxed at only one level—the business owner level. An S corporation's revenues are not taxed at the corporate level; instead, the net revenues of an S corporation are added to the business owner's gross income on her personal income tax return and taxed just once. (Note, however, that the net revenues must be reported and taxed even if the business owners did not distribute those net revenues to themselves.) But the S corporation is still a corporation. It still needs a board of directors and corporate officers and must follow corporate formalities. Therefore, it might not be as agile as a gig economy business would like.

That leads us to the final option: the LLC. The LLC creates the desired liability barrier, is a pass-through tax entity, and doesn't require the legal formalities of a corporation. It's nimble, like your gig economy business, and you will have a lot of flexibility in the way you set up the way you govern the LLC. For these reasons, I suggest the LLC be the preferred choice.

An LLC may have another benefit the others don't: confidentiality. In Virginia, the information required to start an LLC available for public review is minimal. If you don't want the public to guess who owns the LLC, I can draft the legal document in a way that keeps the owners' names out of the public record. This is an important benefit for businesses that don't want clients, vendors, creditors, or anyone else in the public to be able to easily identify and pursue the individual owners.

Using an LLC or a corporation brings credibility to your gig economy business. An LLC or corporation looks professional and makes your business look professional. It is evidence that you are taking your business seriously and that you know what you are doing. You appear to be a serious, long-term venture. Clients and potential clients gain confidence by seeing you use a legal entity for your gig economy business.

YOU MAY HAVE REASONS FOR NOT USING AN LLC.

After all this analysis, however, you might have an important reason to choose an entity other than an LLC.

Years ago, when healthcare laws were different, Phyllis was starting a video production company. She had a serious medical condition that required costly insurance and medication. A C corporation was Phyliss' entity of choice for her unique circumstances so she could obtain and have the business pay for health insurance and medications.

Terri wanted to use a "Rollover Business Startup" to finance her purchase of a franchised business with the money in her 401(k). IRS regulations and guidance required her to use a C corporation in those circumstances.

Chris wanted to use a self-directed individual retirement account (IRA) to fund the startup of his business. The money in the IRA would be used to purchase the equity of the business, resulting in its injection into the business for working capital. While Chris could use an LLC for that business, IRS regulations and guidance required that he elect to have his LLC taxed as a C corporation. So, he ended up with all the benefits of an LLC, except pass-through tax treatment.

Start by choosing the LLC, and then make someone convince you there are special reasons why you should use a different type of entity. If they can't, then you have your answer.

HOW TO START YOUR LLC.

To create your LLC's legal existence, file articles of organization, and pay a filing fee to a state agency. The Articles of Organization is the legal document required to be filed by the state's LLC statute to start the LLC. The statute will indicate the minimum contents of the articles. In Virginia, the articles must include the name of the LLC, its principal office address, the name of its registered agent, and the registered agent's address. Many states have templates of Articles of Organization on their website that you can use as a starting point if you want to try doing it yourself. Some states, like Virginia, also allow for e-filing of Articles of Organization.

Although you can put more information in the articles, I never do for a gig economy business. Why put in more than you are required, especially when changing or deleting that additional information later will require another filing and payment of an additional filing fee?

The state will send you a Certificate of Organization after you have filed acceptable Articles of Organization and paid the filing fee. If your state allows for e-filing, you can draft and file the Articles of Organization, pay the filing fee, and receive your Certificate of Organization immediately. If your state does everything by mail, you might receive your certificate about one to two weeks after you file.

NAMING YOUR LLC.

You need to pick a name for your LLC that is not already used in your state. In Virginia, the statute requires that you choose a name that is "distinguishable upon the records" of the Virginia State Corporation Commission (SCC). You can check your name for distinguishability by using a search function on the SCC's website. Your state might have a similar requirement and search capability.

Even if your LLC name is available in your state's records, however, avoid choosing a name that might infringe upon another company's established name or trademark. Do a quick internet search to see if anyone else is using a similar company name. If they are, determine where they are located, how long they have been in business, and the extent of their geographic market area. In addition, search the US Patent & Trademark Office's online database of trademarks for similar names. Clearing business names can get tricky, so if you are worried that an LLC name you like might have some risk, consult a lawyer to help you analyze that risk before forming an LLC with a questionable name.

CREATE THE LLC IN THE STATE IN WHICH YOUR BUSINESS IS PHYSICALLY LOCATED.

You may hear and see a lot of advice about creating your LLC in a state where your business is not located, like

Wyoming, Nevada, or Delaware. Analyzing that decision is a waste of time for a gig economy business, in my opinion, because the costs and administrative burden of forming an LLC in one of those states usually far outweigh any perceived benefits. If you form your LLC in a state other than where your business is located, you will still need to register or qualify your LLC in your home state. In those circumstances, you will then need to make annual filings and pay annual fees to two states. In addition, you'll need to engage and pay a registered agent in each state. Finally, the state in which you form might require you to maintain a physical presence in that state. There are services you can hire to act as your physical presence, but that's another added cost. You'll have to find a strong reason for creating your LLC in any state other than the one in which you are located.

FOLLOW LEGAL FORMALITIES WHEN SETTING UP YOUR LLC.

To get the full benefit of the liability protection of an LLC you need to do more than file Articles of Organization. You are trying to avoid circumstances that might give a client or creditor the opportunity and ammunition to argue that the liability protection of the LLC should be disregarded so they can get to your personal assets. You may hear the phrase "piercing the corporate veil" used to describe this possibility. You need to follow certain formalities to finish organizing your LLC to decrease a "piercing the veil" risk.

Operating Agreement

After you receive your Certificate of Organization, draft and sign an Operating Agreement for your LLC. The Operating Agreement is a contract between the owners (called "members") that contains provisions identifying the members, their ownership percentages, and their capital contributions. Members of LLCs are not "partners." Referring to a member as a "partner" might cause others to conclude you're operating your gig economy business as a partnership, which could lead to adverse consequences (see the above discussion about why you should avoid running your business as a partnership).

Your gig economy business probably does not need a lot of capital to launch, so consider having each owner make a minimal capital contribution (e.g., $1.00 or $10.00 per percentage point of membership interest) in exchange for her membership interests. Then members can loan the LLC additional funds later if more capital is needed. Note that loans by owners to the LLC are interest-free. Loans from members are also attractive because the Operating Agreement can be drafted to require the payback of those loans before any distribution of net profits is made to the members. Distribution of net profits is ordinary income to a member, which is taxable, while the payback of a loan is not income to the member. Consult a tax professional for more information about this suggested approach.

The Operating Agreement also should contain provisions about how the LLC will be managed, how decisions will be made, prohibitions on selling membership interests in the LLC without consent of the other members, what to do if an owner passes away, and other customary provisions about how to run the business.

Having an Operating Agreement shows the world you are operating the LLC separately from your personal affairs in a manner consistent with best practices and applicable laws. You also will need to show your Operating Agreement to your locality to get a business license and to your bank to open a business bank account. In addition, lenders will ask to see a copy of your Operating Agreement.

Employer Identification Number

Get an Employer Identification Number (EIN) for your LLC from the IRS. The EIN is like a Social Security number for your LLC.

The IRS website has an online EIN application service. Before you start the online EIN application process, however, print a blank Form SS-4 from the IRS's website. The SS-4 is the paper application that can be submitted by mail or fax to apply for an EIN. Even though you will use the online EIN application, I suggest you first fill in the necessary information on the Form SS-4 to use as a guide when you start the online application.

The IRS website will issue an EIN for your LLC upon submission of a properly completed online application. Print the screen that displays your LLC's EIN and save that with your other legal documents. It will act as evidence of your EIN assignment. The IRS also will mail you a letter in a few weeks to confirm the EIN assignment. Keep that letter with your other LLC legal documents as evidence of the EIN.

Note that EINs are not transferable. If you got an EIN to operate your gig economy business as a sole proprietorship or partnership before you started an LLC, the IRS will not allow you to transfer that EIN to your new LLC. You will have to get a new EIN for your LLC.

Business License

Does your locality or state require your LLC to have a business license? If it does, you need to get the license before you start doing business.

Research your state's requirements for business licenses and get one, if necessary. The information should be easy to find on the website of the agency that handles LLC's in your state (usually the Secretary of State or the Corporations Division).

In Virginia, your LLC must get a business license from the city or county in which its principal office is located. The LLC owner must visit the local Commissioner of Revenue's office to apply for the license in person (some Virginia localities allow for online application). The owner needs to bring the Certificate of Organization, Operating Agreement, and EIN. She will complete an application about the business and pay a fee for a one-year license.

Note that a business license might not be transferable. If you got a business license to operate your gig economy business as a sole proprietorship before you started an LLC, you probably cannot transfer that license to your new LLC. You will have to get a new license for the LLC.

Business Bank Account

Part of maintaining the liability barrier to protect your personal assets from your business liabilities is to keep your personal and business money separate. Set up a business checking account at the bank of your choice to handle your business's operating funds. Note that business bank accounts might not have the same terms as personal bank accounts (e.g., you might not get free checking, and there might be transaction fees).

The bank will want to see all the LLC legal documents you have put in place: the Articles of Organization, the Certificate of Organization, the Operating Agreement, the EIN, and the business license (if required). You will need to tell the bank who will be authorized to sign checks and conduct business related to the account.

Deposit the owners' capital contributions and the funds from member loans into the business bank account as soon as possible after the account has been set up.

Do not commingle the funds in your business with your personal funds. Do not pay for personal things using your business account. You risk losing the liability protection of your LLC if you treat the LLC as if it didn't exist.

Other Registrations

Your state might also require you to register your LLC with its state tax department and employment commission or labor department. Find out those requirements by visiting the websites of those agencies.

In Virginia, you must get a state tax identification number for your LLC from the Virginia Department of Taxation. You also must open an account with the Virginia Employment Commission. You can do both at the same time by visiting the Virginia Department of Taxation's website and registering your new business online.

YOU MIGHT NEED INSURANCE.

Judy called for a phone consultation about setting up a new LLC. She is a certified Pilates instructor. Pilates training is her side business, but she plans to turn it into her full-time business. A friend suggested she set up an LLC. She called me to discuss what protection an LLC might provide. During our conversation, we discussed that physical injuries to her clients were her most significant risk. Judy explained she had insurance to cover that risk.

No legal entity will protect you from your negligent acts or omissions. The liability barrier is disregarded when an owner is negligent. That's why physicians, dentists, lawyers, architects, engineers, and accountants have malpractice insurance. They can't avoid liability for their malpractice (another word for negligence) by delivering their services using a legal entity.

What's the nature of your business and the services or products you will provide? Is there a possibility a client might claim you were negligent? Could your alleged negligence injure someone or cause damage to their business? For instance, are you a cybersecurity consultant? Do you train military or law enforcement on firearm tactics? Are you a physician providing healthcare services on a contract basis to assisted living facilities? Are you performing data analytics for your clients as an independent contractor? Are you a personal trainer?

If the nature of your services or products might expose you to negligence claims, you probably need liability insurance (e.g., errors and omissions insurance or malpractice insurance). Consult with an insurance professional to help you identify potential risks and insurance products that could cover those risks. Some industry associations also offer insurance products to their members, sometimes at a discount. If your industry has such an association, research their insurance products and consider joining (if you are not already a member) to take advantage of that benefit.

The need for insurance does not negate the benefits of an LLC for your business: it's just added protection to cover a risk your LLC cannot protect you against.

GET A BUSINESS LAWYER TO HELP YOU IF YOU HAVE LEGAL QUESTIONS OR AREN'T COMFORTABLE HANDLING THESE TASKS.

Most gig economy businesses I represent are owned by fiercely independent people who like to do as much as they can themselves. I'm the same way. But a smart business owner knows when he is out of his swim lane and should get professional help.

Starting a gig economy business requires dealing with a lot of legal issues. Many business lawyers offer reasonably priced startup business packages to handle these legal issues and tasks for you. For example, my LLC formation package includes a consultation about choice of entity and other startup questions, LLC name clearance search, drafting and filing Articles of Organization, drafting the Operating Agreement, obtaining the EIN, and delivering an LLC formation packet to my client ready to be signed and used to get a business license and open a business banking account. The fees for this service are less expensive than the time you would need to research and educate yourself on how to identify and resolve these issues and complete the legal tasks associated with starting an LLC. Plus, you get the benefit of the lawyer's experience and expertise.

2

INTELLECTUAL PROPERTY

YOU HAVE SKILLS, KNOW-HOW, IDEAS, concepts, methods, processes, formulae, recipes, and maybe even previously created work. These items have great value. You will use them when you perform services to create deliverables and work product for your clients. Many times, that's what you're selling, and its why your client wants to engage you. Having a basic understanding of intellectual property issues and how they work in a gig economy business setting is crucial to your survival.

WHAT IS INTELLECTUAL PROPERTY?

Many years ago, when intellectual property law was just starting to blossom, the Intellectual Property section of my local bar organization held a luncheon where a popular business consultant was the featured speaker. She began her remarks with a serious question: Why did we call ourselves "smart real estate lawyers"? Apparently, no one took the time to determine whether she knew what the term "intellectual property" meant, so she took her best guess. Her comment was awkward for everyone in attendance. The following explanation will hopefully spare you the embarrassment that speaker experienced.

You need to know what intellectual property is and how to protect it if you have a gig economy business because your services likely will use assets and result in work product that is protected by intellectual property laws. The ownership of intellectual property involved in your projects can become the hottest issue in your relationships with clients.

Copyrights, trademarks, trade secrets, and patents are commonly referred to as "intellectual property." I'll refer to intellectual property for the rest of this book as "IP."

The intangibles you bring to a client's project probably are protected by law. You might write software code, develop written marketing or business plans, design an app or website, analyze data and create reports, develop IT architecture, design logos, design graphics for websites or data visualization, create or modify training programs, or even shoot photographs or videos, or compose and record music. These types of output are protected by copyright law.

If you create names for products, slogans, or logos, these types of output are protected by trademark law.

If you develop a secret method, algorithm, formula, analysis, marketing or business plan, financial projections, proposed budget, or anything else that derives value from being kept secret, these types of output are protected by trade secret law.

If you invent something novel and useful, it might be protected by patent law.

These examples aren't exhaustive; there are many more types of output that might fit into one or another category of intellectual property.

WHY SHOULD I CARE ABOUT IP?

Jan developed a software application for analyzing financial data to identify opportunities for businesses to increase profits by modifying sales force behavior based on the results of the analyses. Jan developed the logic and algorithms coded into the software application, which are confidential. Employees for Jan's business designed and coded the software application.

Jan offers two categories of consulting services. One service involves the client providing financial data to Jan's business, with Jan then crunching the numbers in her office using her software application and providing periodic reports and recommendations to her client. The second service involves the installation of the software application on the client's server, training the client's employees how to use the software, and working with the client to ensure things are going smoothly.

Jan's services and software make millions for her clients. Protecting Jan's IP protects her ability to do business.

Jan's software code is protected by copyright law. The logic and algorithms coded into the application are trade secrets. Jan's experience and know-how have tremendous value and are also trade secrets.

Jan's clients, especially those who buy the second category of services, are well-aware of the value of Jan's IP. That's why they engage her business. The ownership of that IP and what Jan can do with it are the most hotly negotiated issues when Jan engages a new client. Some clients want to own the software (and the logic and algorithms contained in it), and some clients just want to maintain a competitive advantage by preventing Jan from taking on their competitors as clients.

Jan diligently guards her company's ownership of its IP through confidentiality agreements and consulting agreements that contain carefully worded provisions about what IP Jan's company retains and what IP her client will own. Without those protections, Jan's business would die because it would lose its most valuable assets.

Your IP might also be your gig economy business's most valuable asset. Figure out what your IP is, what value it has, and how you are going to protect it when you release it into your clients' hands. If you don't, you will quickly learn how valuable a client considers your IP when they claim they own it.

DETERMINE WHAT IP YOU OWN.

Take an inventory of your IP. What have you created that you will bring to the table when you perform services and create work product for your clients? What do you need to hold on to so you can keep providing services to clients?

A book cannot identify your IP for you, but the following are some examples of IP my clients have. Consider whether you have anything similar:

- Expert knowledge based on your experiences and training;
- Knowledge of little known methods or techniques;
- A library of software code you have developed that can be plugged into new applications;
- Self-produced training programs and student materials;
- Process logic that few, if any, others know;
- Original algorithms;
- Original application of existing logic or algorithms;
- The identity of a chemical and its manufacturing source;
- The unique use of a well-known chemical;
- Graphic designs that are your original work;
- A unique, distinguishable, and recognizable graphic art style;
- Original formula or process for analyzing data;
- Stock photography, graphic images, or videography you created;
- Marketing or business plan templates;
- A compliance handbook you wrote;
- A recipe for creating customized materials (e.g., semiconductors);

- An original advertising campaign you developed as a template; or
- A technical manual you wrote.

The list is as long as people are creative.

Consult with a lawyer with IP law experience for professional help and guidance to identify your IP, to assess its value to your gig economy business, and to determine how to protect it.

HOW DO I PROTECT MY "TOOLKIT"?

My father was a specialty general contractor with clients mostly in the Georgetown neighborhood of Washington, DC. Even though Georgetown residents are very wealthy, crime can be an issue in that neighborhood, even during the day. My father had a van full of tools he had purchased over a long period of time. Some tools had been purchased to do specific jobs, while others were more pedestrian but still necessary. He took precautions to secure and protect his tools. The van had few windows, so it was difficult to see the van's contents. He kept the van locked at all times, even while on a job site. If the job required multiple trips to the van for tools and materials, the van would be unlocked and then locked after each trip. One of my father's competitors even kept a Doberman Pinscher in his van. My father's protection of his tools protected his ability to make a living.

If you are a gig economy worker, you have tools, too. Your tools might consist of your expertise, know-how, and other IP you have developed. You need those tools to perform your services and make a living. If my father lost a tool or had it stolen (or even gave it away), he could always replace it by purchasing another. Your tools are different. You can't purchase new tools once yours are gone. If you sell, give away, or lose your tools, you lose the ability to make a living.

Clients might not understand your need to protect your toolkit. Their lawyer may have told them they should obtain ownership of everything you do for them. You might have to educate your clients during the contract negotiation period about why you need to retain ownership of certain things they think they are buying from you.

Protecting your toolkit starts with identifying your IP. Once you have done that, you need to determine how to protect your tools and how they will be incorporated into the deliverables you create for a client.

Certain tools obtain enhanced protection through registration. You can register copyrights for software code, graphic images, photographs, videos, handbooks, manuals, books, or other digital or written materials you have produced to be used in the performance of your services. Also, use a proper copyright notice on those materials. A copyright notice tells the world you own the material and are serious about protecting your ownership. Consult the US Copyright Office's online guidance or an intellectual property lawyer for the requirements of a copyright notice.

Mark confidential information "Confidential." Keep it secure (e.g., password protect documents containing confidential information and make only limited hard copies). A good practice is to number confidential hard copies, keep them under lock and key if possible, restrict their distribution to only those who need to know, and keep a record of who possesses them. Also make sure your contracts with clients require your clients to keep your confidential information confidential, even after your engagement has ended.

Finally, make sure your contracts with your clients contain language clearly indicating you retain ownership of your toolkit. Some clients might balk at that language because aspects of your toolkit might be incorporated into the work product resulting from your services. If that is true, there is a simple solution that should satisfy most clients. In your contract, grant them a "non-exclusive, perpetual, royalty-free, non-transferable, worldwide license" to use your tools only in connection with the work product in which they are incorporated. Then they have what they need.

If, after all you have done to make your client happy while protecting your toolkit, your client still insists on owning your IP, you have to make a business-changing decision. Either drop the client or sell them your IP. If you offer to sell your IP to your client, you can drive your point home about the value of your IP by pricing it so high that the client realizes the license described in the preceding paragraph is the better approach (e.g., base your suggested price on the present value of lost future earnings over the predicted life of your business).

HOW DO I KEEP A PROSPECT
FROM TAKING MY IDEAS?

Rodriguez Advertising was the hot new advertising agency on the block in my city. It was founded and run by a hip young man with a lot of flair. The agency had recently won a prestigious award from a national advertising industry magazine as one of the best new agencies in the Southeast.

A national bank asked Rodriguez Advertising to pitch a new ad campaign. The bank refused to sign a confidentiality agreement. They explained that they received so many proposals in response to their solicitations that it would be too burdensome to keep track of which proposal was covered by which confidentiality agreement. Rodriguez asked me what to do to help protect their ideas and proposal.

I recommended Rodriguez Advertising prominently mark its proposal "CONFIDENTIAL." I also recommended it include a copyright notice on its proposal. Rodriguez did not follow my recommendations.

Rodriguez pitched its ideas for the advertising campaign but didn't get the contract. Instead, a much larger ad agency won the contract. When the ad campaign was launched, it closely resembled the campaign Rodriguez pitched. Rodriguez believed the bank had given the other ad agency a copy of Rodriguez's proposal. Rodriguez had lost not only the pitch contest but also its ideas. They might have been able to sue the bank and the other ad agency for misappropriation, but it would have been a difficult, expensive, and time-consuming case to litigate. Rodriguez decided not to pursue the claim.

In a perfect world, the best way to keep a prospective client from taking ideas you share during the pitch phase is to have the prospect sign a confidentiality agreement before you make your pitch. I suggest my clients use a short, easy-to-understand evaluation confidentiality agreement indicating that my client is disclosing confidential information to the prospect for the sole purpose of evaluating whether to enter into a contractual relationship. It obligates the prospect to keep the information confidential, to not use it for any purpose other than evaluating the potential business relationship, and to return all confidential information upon my client's request or if they decide not to engage my client. It covers all confidential information you disclose for the pitch, whether verbally or in writing, even if that information was disclosed before the confidentiality agreement was signed.

A prospective client might take the confidentiality agreement idea up a notch. The prospect might also disclose its confidential information to you to help you prepare your pitch. In that event, the prospect may ask you to sign a confidentiality agreement. That's fine. Just make sure it's mutual; that it runs both ways, protecting the prospect's confidential information and your confidential information. Your prospect may even have a form of mutual non-disclosure and confidentiality agreement they want you to sign. Again, that's fine, as long as you confirm that it provides the protection you require. I recommend getting a lawyer's input on any contract presented to you before you sign it.

Some businesses won't sign a confidentiality agreement for a proposal or pitch. In my experience, this is a common practice among large companies. In those instances, they will ask you to trust them. It's a risk. Reduce that risk by prominently marking your materials (including presentation slides) as "confidential." Also, include a proper copyright notice on your materials. In addition, carefully consider what confidential information you will include in your proposal or pitch. Perhaps you can tease some information, rather than disclosing all of it. Lastly, if you are not chosen for the project, ask the prospect in an email or letter to return the information, or to certify they have destroyed the proposal or pitch materials. Then, keep your eyes and ears open to observe whether the prospect or the contractor who won the job appears to be using your ideas.

WHO OWNS THE WORK PRODUCT YOU CREATE FOR A CLIENT?

A partner at the law firm I worked for called me to his office one morning about a problem his client was having with a contractor. The client was a national bank. It had engaged a freelance software developer to create custom software the bank could use to transfer money between branches electronically (this was almost 25 years ago before such software was widely available and in use). The developer worked in the bank's office because he needed access to the bank's servers and personnel for development and testing purposes.

Over one weekend, the bank's IT personnel reviewed the contractor's work to evaluate his progress. They discovered the contractor had inserted code into the application that caused the software to scan the list of authorized users each time the software was launched. The code would shut down the software if the contractor's name was not on that list.

The bank was furious. When the contractor returned to the bank's office on Monday, he was met by a security guard and a bank officer. His contract was immediately terminated. The security guard escorted the contractor to his work area and allowed the contractor a few minutes to clear out his desk. The security guard then escorted the contractor from the building.

Later that day, the contractor contacted the bank to inform them that they did not have the right to use the software because he owned the copyright to it. He offered to sell the bank a license to use the software. That's when the bank called its law firm.

I asked to review a copy of the bank's contract with the developer. It was short and poorly drafted. It was obvious no lawyer with IP law experience had drafted or even reviewed it. I was looking for specific language about the ownership of the software application. There was none. We called the bank back that afternoon and recommended they pay the license fee (which was actually a reasonable amount), which they did.

Work under the assumption that you own everything you create for a client. Much of the work product developed by gig economy businesses for clients is protected by copyright law. Software code, website design, website content, graphic images, handbooks, training materials, curricula, tests, marketing plans, business plans, and advertising campaign proposals are just some examples of work product protected by copyright. The US Copyright Act indicates that the creator of a protected work is the owner. In certain narrow circumstances, the work product might be considered "work-made-for-hire," but those circumstances usually don't encompass a gig economy business's work product.

"Work-made-for-hire" is a widely misunderstood concept. Many businesses and contractors believe that as long as the contract says the work product is "work-made-for-hire," that's enough to transfer ownership from the contractor to the client. It's not.

The Copyright Act defines "work-made-for-hire" as (1) work created by an employee for her employer within the scope of her employment, or (2) a few specific types of work product (e.g., a contribution to a collective work, part of a motion picture or other audiovisual work, a translation, a supplementary work, a compilation, an instructional text, a test, answer material for a test, or an atlas) if the contract contains language specifically indicating that the work product is "work-made-for-hire." Most gig economy business work product does not fall within either of these definitions, so the contractor retains ownership of the work product, even if the contract indicates it is "work-made-for-hire."

The better and customary practice is to include two provisions in the client's contract. The first provision should clearly identify what the work product will be. The second provision should indicate that the work product is "work-made-for-hire," but also that to the extent the work product is not "work-made-for-hire," as defined in the US Copyright Act, the contractor is assigning to the client all right, title, interest, and copyright in and to the work product. (Remember to carve out the retention of the ownership to your toolkit from that transfer.) That should be sufficient to make your client comfortable that it is getting the ownership rights it desires.

Even if the work product is not protected by copyright law, using the same types of contractual provisions about the ownership of work product (perhaps with a little tweaking to indicate that it applies to all forms of IP) is customary.

Note that a well-versed client also might ask you to promise you will sign additional documents it requests to evidence the transfer of work product ownership. Those agreements might include a stand-alone assignment document. This too is customary, and should not create a lot of concern or negotiation. Beware of language that gives your client the right to sign documents on your behalf (e.g., a power of attorney) if you don't sign and return them quickly enough. You don't want to give your client the unilateral right to determine what documents it needs without your review, and then sign them without your knowledge.

What if the contract doesn't use the language I suggest above, but uses some other language indicating who owns the work product and associated intellectual property rights? I have reviewed contracts that simply say: "The client shall own all work product and associated intellectual property rights." Is that contractual language just as good as what I suggest above? I don't think so. Even if a court would enforce that language, who wants to go to court for an interpretation when you can clearly indicate ownership in your written contract when you are drafting it? It's easy to avoid the time and cost of interpreting an ambiguous contract provision by using well-established enforceable contract language at the beginning of the client relationship, so do that instead of taking the risk of creating a future dispute by relying on non-conforming contractual language.

CAN I USE WORK PRODUCT PRODUCED FOR ONE CLIENT ON A PROJECT FOR ANOTHER CLIENT?

While developing a website for a pool services business, Juan's gig economy business codes a feature into the website that allows customers to schedule service appointments online. He also codes a feature that allows customers to sign up for or renew annual subscriptions for pool maintenance services. Juan realizes these features might be advantageous for businesses in other industries, such as heating and air conditioning businesses, lawn maintenance businesses, and car detailing businesses. He wants to retain the right to use the software code for those features to build websites for other businesses that take customer appointments and offer subscriptions for their services. Juan realizes he might be able to increase his profit margin and decrease the time needed to develop a website for these businesses if he can use the previously created code.

The contract between your client and your gig economy business will answer the question about whether you can use work product created for one client in connection with projects for other clients. If the contract transfers ownership of your work product to your client, then you probably will not be able to use that work product on a project for another client. This is especially true if the work product is protected by intellectual property law (e.g., trademark, copyright, trade secret, or patent) or if the work product is included within the contract's definition of the client's confidential information.

If the work product is of a general nature that is well known in your industry, it might not be protected by intellectual property law or confidentiality restrictions. This is a delicate decision to make, especially unilaterally, so I highly recommend you obtain a lawyer's advice before you decide to use work product for another project.

The risk you take in using work product from one project for a different client is being accused of misappropriation of trade secrets (if the work product is a trade secret), breach of contract (e.g., for breaching the confidentiality restrictions of your contract), intellectual property infringement (e.g., copyright infringement), or a combination of these claims. These are serious risks that could destroy your business.

If you think you might want to use work product from one project for future projects (even if they are unknown at the time), bring this issue up with your client during contract negotiations. Putting this issue on the table early will set expectations with your client and help you achieve your objective of obtaining some right to use certain work product in the future. Clearly drafting your rights to use work product into your client contract also will reduce the possibility of future disputes over work product usage. If your client agrees, you eliminate the risks outlined above.

If you don't realize until sometime into a project that you are creating work product you might want to use for projects for other clients, approach your current client and communicate the issue and your objective to them. Be particularly clear about how you will use that work product in the future. Explain why your use of that work product will not reduce your current client's competitive advantage or infringe on the intellectual property rights it is obtaining from you. You might agree to not use the work product for a business in the same industry as your current client within its geographic market area. If your current client agrees to your proposal, draft the agreement into a written amendment to your current contract and have your client sign it (you sign it, too).

CAN I USE WORK PRODUCT FOR MY PORTFOLIO?

John's gig economy business develops websites. Monique's business creates graphic images to visualize data. Paul's gig economy business develops customized, confidential software for businesses. Jodie's business shoots photographs for commercial use (e.g., in magazines, annual reports for businesses, and business websites). Craig's business shoots videos for commercial use (e.g., on business websites and YouTube channels). In each instance, ownership of the work product created by these gig economy businesses is transferred to the client.

John, Monique, Paul, Jodie, and Craig market their gig economy services by showing potential clients the great work they have done for other clients. They collect examples of their work into portfolios and online galleries. Some of that work, such as publicly available websites and published photographs, can be shared with anyone without any risk because it already is publicly accessible. John, Monique, Paul, Jodie, and Craig will need specific permission from the client for whom the work product was created to include copies of other types of work product into their portfolio if that work product is confidential.

Do not assume you have the right to use work product in your portfolio. Making that assumption might result in a breach of your client's confidentiality restrictions or intellectual property rights. If you want to use work product created for a client in your portfolio, include that right in your written contract. Make it a matter of practice to have a provision in your template client contract for that purpose. Your client might want to negotiate certain limitations on the use of work product in your portfolio, such as blurring out certain images or including a copyright notice showing that your client owns the copyright to a graphic image, and that's probably reasonable.

3

CONTRACTING WITH CLIENTS

YOU'LL HAVE WONDERFUL CLIENTS AND difficult clients. The difficult clients create risks for your gig economy business. These risks include the risk of not getting paid, the risk of your client claiming you didn't adequately perform your services, the risk of your client demanding a refund, the risk of your client claiming ownership of your ideas, know-how, expertise, and creations, the risk of having to litigate a dispute in a different state or country, and the risk of not getting your lawyer's fees paid or reimbursed if you win a lawsuit against a client.

You will enter into a contractual relationship with each of your clients. That contract, in whatever form it takes, will govern your interaction with each client. Make a conscious effort to create a good contract. Good contracts lead to good client relationships and good results. Adopt a contract-making process at the beginning of your gig economy business and stick to it. Doing so will reduce your risks.

ARE YOU AN INDEPENDENT
CONTRACTOR OR AN EMPLOYEE?

Jeff installed floors in office buildings. Angelo's company found all the jobs, designed and estimated the jobs, purchased all the flooring materials, determined Jeff's work schedule, collected all the money from the building owners, determined Jeff's fees for his work, paid for Jeff's travel, lodging, and meal expenses, and paid Jeff for his services on a bi-weekly basis. Jeff used his own truck to do the work, but Angelo would purchase any specialty tools Jeff needed for a job (which Jeff could then keep on his truck). Jeff didn't perform his services for anyone other than Angelo's company. There was no written contract between Jeff and Angelo's company, and Jeff did not invoice Angelo's company for his work. Angelo considered Jeff an independent contractor and paid him as such, rather than as an employee. But was Jeff really an independent contractor, or was he an employee in disguise?

Will you be an independent contractor to your clients when you start up your gig economy business? Or will you be deemed an employee, even though your client and you try to make you look like an independent contractor? And why does it matter?

Let's start with why it matters. Employers must pay payroll taxes on employee wages and salaries. Employees also pay a portion of their wages or salaries as taxes. If an employer engages an independent contractor to perform services, the employer is not required to pay payroll taxes on the fees it pays to the independent contractor. Likewise, the independent contractor will not be required to contribute a portion of its fees to pay payroll taxes on the fees it receives from its client. Not having to pay payroll taxes can be a significant saving for an employer and an independent contractor.

Employers also provide benefits to employees, such as health insurance and contributions to retirement plans. Clients do not provide employee benefits to independent contractors. This is another way a company can save money by using an independent contractor instead of an employee.

Not having to pay payroll taxes or provide employee benefits are incentives for employers to classify a worker as an independent contractor. Why not terminate an employee and then immediately engage her as an independent contractor for the same services she was performing while an employee? Or, why not instead engage all workers as independent contractors? These practices are common in some industries but can have serious financial consequences.

The IRS and state tax agencies and labor departments are well aware of the practice to characterize workers as independent contractors instead of employees. As a result, they have adopted policies, regulations, and tests to confirm the classification of workers as independent contractors or employees. Misclassification could financially destroy your gig economy business. If you are misclassified as an independent contractor when you are really an employee, then you might have to pay back taxes, interest, and civil penalties when discovered by the IRS or state agency.

Look at the IRS guidance to determine whether you are being correctly classified as an independent contractor in your relationship with a client. Several examples of this include, if you have only one client and it provides you with the equivalent of a full-time amount of work, if you receive employee-like benefits (e.g., paid time off), if the client provides the tools, supplies, office space, computer, and software for you, and if you're not working on a project-by-project basis (i.e., your relationship continues even after you finish a project), then the IRS and state tax agencies likely will ignore your assertion that you are an independent contractor, even if you have a contract that says so.

This whole discussion also applies to your engagement of subcontractors. Set up those relationships so your subcontractors will be classified as independent contractors, rather than your employees. Doing so will avoid the risks of misclassification.

USE A WRITTEN CONTRACT.

Working without a written contract is like doing trapeze without a net. It's very risky should something go wrong. And, unfortunately, things go wrong in client-contractor relationships more often than you might expect.

Verbal contracts are enforceable, but they are difficult to enforce. If a dispute arises between your client and you, it will be your word against theirs. It's unlikely you and your client will agree on what the terms of the agreement are— you're already in a dispute! It will take a court to untangle the verbal agreement, and that takes time (including time away from your business) and money and creates stress. Why would you take on that risk at the beginning of a client relationship?

Create a client onboarding process by which you introduce a contract to them at the beginning of the relationship as a matter of course. Then get that contract finalized and signed before you begin your work.

Your written contract will be the roadmap for your client relationship. Both your client and you can refer back to it when questions about the relationship arise. It will form the basis for resolving disputes. A well-written contract might even keep you out of court because your client and you might be more willing to negotiate a resolution when one or both of you see that the contract has provisions relevant to the disputed issue.

Using a written contract establishes credibility with your clients. That practice impresses upon them that you have carefully considered how you want to define the relationship in a professional manner.

A written contract can improve your lawyer's ability to resolve a dispute. She will be able to review the contract and advise you on possible resolutions, develop a strategy for resolving the dispute, and predict your likelihood of winning. She also may be able to use provisions in the contract to negotiate a resolution with your client (or its lawyer) without the need for a lawsuit.

If you don't have a written contract and a dispute arises, you don't give your lawyer anything to work with other than your side of the story, which your client is sure to reject in favor of their own.

It's a red flag if a potential client doesn't think a written contract is necessary. Saving on some legal fees is not a good enough reason to take on the risks of a verbal agreement.

A PROPOSAL IS NOT A CONTRACT.

Catherine's consulting business routinely provides written proposals to prospective clients. Her practice is to have clients accept the proposal by signing it. Catherine then proceeds to do the work. Is Catherine's accepted proposal a contract with her client? Maybe. The proposal might be a contract if it contains all the elements the law requires. Or, it might not be a contract, if it lacks any of those elements.

Even if an accepted proposal constitutes a contract, it's probably a poor one. Rarely do I see proposals that contain the necessary provisions of a gig economy contract (see below), which means you are leaving yourself exposed to lots of risks if you use proposals as contracts.

The better practice is to build into your proposal the requirement that a prospective client will sign your template client contract when it accepts the proposal. You should provide your prospect with a copy of your contract when you deliver the proposal so it can review the contract at the same time it considers your proposal.

ALWAYS GET THE CONTRACT SIGNED.

Betty's business sells and installs cabinets and shelving for commercial and residential garage organization. The cabinets and shelving are covered by a manufacturer's warranty. The manufacturer has environmental specifications for the cabinets and shelving, such as temperature and humidity limits, weight limits, and prohibitions on the types of materials stored. If a customer doesn't comply with the specifications, the manufacturer's warranty is voided.

Betty issues a purchase order to each client. The purchase order has terms and conditions printed on the back that pass the manufacturer's warranty through to the client and require the client to acknowledge and agree to comply with the manufacturer's specifications. The terms and conditions also disclaim any implied warranties about the cabinets and shelving.

One of Betty's clients experienced failures with cabinets and shelving. When the client submitted its claim to the manufacturer, the manufacturer discovered the client had not complied with the environmental specifications. As a result, the manufacturer voided the warranty and rejected the warranty claim. Betty's client thinks Betty's company should be responsible for the broken cabinets and shelving.

When Betty brought this problem to me, I asked to review the contract she entered into with her client. Betty shared the purchase order with me. While the purchase order contained all the provisions described above, it was not signed by the client. In fact, I discovered Betty never had any clients sign a purchase order—she simply issued the purchase order. Without a client's signature, it would be difficult to prove the client saw and agreed to the terms and conditions about the manufacturer's warranty, the environmental specifications, and Betty's warranty disclaimers. While a contract exists between Betty's company and its clients, that contract probably would not include the terms and conditions on the back of Betty's purchase order.

Kenneth operated a retail store in leased space in a shopping center. He had several years left on his lease. A popular national restaurant franchise contacted Kenneth's landlord about leasing Kenneth's space for a new restaurant. The landlord met with Kenneth to negotiate an early termination to the lease so he could get that restaurant into his shopping center. Kenneth was eager to end the lease early, too, because his business was suffering.

The landlord and Kenneth seemed to reach an agreement during their meeting. The landlord asked me to draft up an early termination agreement. I did so the next day and emailed it to the landlord. While the landlord acknowledged in emails that he was still interested in terminating Kenneth's lease early, the landlord never signed the early termination agreement. Against my advice, Kenneth decided to close his store and move out of the space, relying on the landlord's emails.

The landlord was unable to get the restaurant to sign a lease. The landlord then sued Kenneth for unpaid rent and won. The court would not enforce the verbal agreement made during the meeting because the landlord didn't sign the early termination agreement. The court also explained that the landlord's emails about early termination were not the same as a signature on the agreement.

Sal's company develops and licenses a software application for creating task lists. Sal's website contains the terms and conditions of its license agreement, but Sal's company has no process for obtaining a subscriber's electronic signature to the agreement. One of Sal's customers stopped paying its license fees but kept using a copy of the software. Sal asked me how to collect the license fees or stop the customer from using the software. I couldn't use Sal's terms and conditions as the basis of my settlement negotiations because Sal couldn't prove the customer ever agreed to them.

Each of these examples illustrates different ways in which you can get in trouble if you don't get your client to sign your contract. Without your client's signature, you might not have a contract, or, even if you have an enforceable verbal contract or an implied contract, it won't contain the terms and conditions in your template client contract. Instead, the law might impose terms and conditions that are detrimental to you, such as implied warranties of merchantability and fitness for a particular purpose.

Get your client's signature on your contract. Don't start work without it.

In this digital age, most business, including contract formation, is done over the internet. That's expected and efficient. Laws exist that allow for electronic signatures on contracts or for digital processes that are the equivalent of a signature. If you decide to use an electronic signature process, however, consult a lawyer to ensure your process creates an enforceable signature on your contracts.

DECIDE WHICH TYPE OF WRITTEN CONTRACT FITS YOUR BUSINESS AND YOUR CLIENTS.

Written contracts come in many shapes, sizes, lengths, and forms. The type of contract you choose will depend on a number of factors, including the type of services you offer, the amount of fees you will be paid, how your services are delivered, the size of your potential client's business, and what's customary in your industry.

Written contracts can take the form of a formal paper contract, a letter agreement, terms and conditions printed on the back of a purchase order, or online terms and conditions, just to name a few examples. No lawyer or online do-it-yourself legal document preparation service can tell you which type of written contract will work well for your gig economy business without first knowing about your business and your potential clients.

Tania's business provides human resources consulting services on multiple projects to an international manufacturing company. Both sides want a formal written contract that contains comprehensive and thoroughly negotiated provisions to define their relationship in detail.

Zach's business provides data analytic services to Fortune 500 companies. Both sides want a formal, thoroughly negotiated written contract before Zach's company starts its work.

Julie's business provides yoga instruction to individual clients at her home studio. Julie has each client sign a one-page, non-negotiable personal training contract setting out the terms and conditions of the relationship.

Rodney's business provides custom cabinet installation services. The purchase order for cabinets and installation services contains a printed set of terms and conditions on the back. Both the client and Rodney sign the purchase order before materials are ordered and work begins.

Maria is a lawyer with a virtual law office. She provides legal services to clients throughout her state. She does not have a brick-and-mortar office; she works from home and handles all of her projects over the Internet. Maria's website contains a set of terms and conditions for engaging her. A client who wants to hire Maria for a project must click-through her terms and conditions to "sign" her online engagement agreement.

Each of the above are examples of different forms of written contracts that fit the clients, the projects, and the industries. Before you engage your first client, adopt a form of written contract (called a "template client contract" in this book) you will use as the baseline for your engagements, then use it, even if it's just a starting point.

Start by looking at what your competitors do (although if they don't use written contracts, don't follow their examples). Review their contracts to see what they contain if you can. Then get help from a lawyer with experience drafting, reviewing, and negotiating gig economy business contracts.

WHAT IF YOUR CLIENT PRESENTS YOU WITH ITS CONTRACT?

The bigger the client, the more likely it will have a template client contract it wants to use, even if you have your own. A client that has an internal legal department likely will have a process it uses for engaging independent contractors that includes a template contract. Zach's data analytics business described above often encounters this client approach because he regularly works for Fortune 500 companies that have an internal legal department, and a process for hiring independent contractors.

Your client's template contract probably addresses the same issues your template client contract addresses, except in a way that is much more favorable to your client. For example, your client's contract might contain a strict process for getting paid. It also might transfer ownership of all intellectual property rights in your work product (including your expertise, know-how, and previously created works) to your client. In addition, it might contain dispute resolution procedures that favor your client.

What can you do in this situation?

First, don't be offended. Your client's process is not a reflection of you. It's usually a product of many years of good and bad experiences your client has had with other independent contractors.

You could push back by ignoring your client's template contract by sending (or re-sending) your template client contract, but that approach usually isn't well-received.

Instead, view your client's template contract as a starting point and an invitation to negotiate. Work to negotiate into that contract your important issues. Also, work to temper client-favorable provisions by educating your client on why those provisions need to be more reasonable.

It's a red flag, however, if your client is unwilling to negotiate any aspect of its template contract. Don't be lulled into signing a non-negotiable contract by a client's verbal promises that it won't follow certain provisions of the contract or it will do more than what's stated in the contract. Well-written contracts contain a provision indicating that the written agreement supersedes all verbal promises.

COMMON PROBLEMS WITH POORLY DRAFTED CONTRACTS.

The contract you sign with your client will become the binding legal document that will control your work and relationship. Everyone will refer to the contract to resolve disputes that arise during and after the project. If the contract is well-drafted, then you will minimize the risk of legal disputes and maximize the possibility of clear and fair resolutions. A well-drafted contract will provide certainty and predictability.

You and your client will verbally negotiate and agree on the significant terms of the deal before you put them into a written contract. As a result, clients and gig economy businesses often view the contract as a mere formality. This causes the client and the gig economy business to downplay the contract, which sets them up for problems later.

The general problems I describe below spring from the client's and the gig economy business's decision to take shortcuts when drafting the contract. Sometimes they take shortcuts because they believe the shortcuts will save on legal fees. Other times, they take shortcuts because they believe the deal is so friendly that a detailed contract is not necessary. Still other times, the parties take shortcuts because they believe drafting and negotiating a contract will take too much time, especially if lawyers are involved. Shortcuts create risks.

You and your lawyer should be on the lookout for problems with the contract before you sign it. These problems include using someone else's template client contract that doesn't fit the deal, ambiguity in the contract, undefined words, agreements to agree, and verbal agreements not reflected in writing. Each of these problems is further explained below.

Using Someone Else's Template Client Contract

Gig economy businesses and their clients sometimes use someone else's template client contract because they believe it will help them save on legal fees. You can find examples of contracts online. There are even online services that sell templates for a modest price. Or, you may be able to get a copy of a contract from someone else in your industry. Many gig economy businesses believe they can simply print up one of these templates, fill in the blanks, get their client to sign it, and move forward.

The biggest problem with using someone else's contract is that the contract doesn't fit your deal. It usually leaves out important aspects. That means the binding contract you signed does not contain the same deal you verbally negotiated. And you will be stuck with what the written contract says about the deal.

Another problem with someone else's contract is that you have no idea how up-to-date the contract is. That contract may have been drafted many years ago. Outdated contracts may not comply with current law. In addition, an outdated contract might fail to address circumstances that didn't exist when the contract was drafted. For example, the contract might fail to transfer intellectual property rights properly, which could cause a big problem for you and your clients.

Contracts are governed by state law. Someone else's contract might have been drafted for use in another state. In that instance, the contract might have provisions that are unenforceable in your state (or enforced or interpreted differently).

Some gig economy businesses believe they can save on legal fees by drafting their template client contract using someone else's contract as a starting point, and then having their lawyer review and tweak it. I had a client take this approach. She allowed her customer to put together a contract using a form found on the internet. My client brought the template contract to me for a quick review. The contract was so poorly drafted, I had to re-draft most of the provisions in the contract. My client spent more legal fees taking this approach then she would have spent had she simply asked me to draft a template client contract for her.

Your lawyer probably has her own starting point for drafting a template client contract—her own particular template. But your lawyer's template should be much better than anything you find online, because your lawyer is a licensed professional and has refined her template from years of doing gig economy deals. When your lawyer uses her template as the starting point, you get the benefit of all of her experience from previous deals without having to pay legal fees for it.

Even if your client's lawyer drafts the contract, you still get the benefit of starting with a contract drafted by a lawyer. Your lawyer's review of that contract should not require a significant re-writing. Instead, your lawyer will be more focused on making sure the contract reflects your understanding of the terms of the deal and contains customary and reasonable protections for you, as the contractor.

The primary purpose of having a lawyer represent you in the deal is to make sure your contract is enforceable and adequately protects you. You will avoid the risk of having provisions of your contract be unenforceable when a lawyer (whether yours or the clients) drafts the contract. That peace of mind is well worth the legal fees you will pay.

Ambiguity

You want to be able to look to the contract for answers to help you resolve any dispute that arises between you and your client. If the contract is ambiguous, then you will not be able to resolve the dispute without a lawsuit or arbitration. Lawsuits and arbitrations cost a lot of money and time, and the outcome is always uncertain.

Ambiguity means not only that a word or phrase is unclear, but also that a word or phrase might be subject to multiple interpretations. For example, the term "monthly payments" in a contract can have multiple meanings without further explanation. What day are the payments due? Are the payments to be equal, or is any payment during a month satisfactory?

Another common area for ambiguity in a gig economy contract is the description of services and deliverables. Indicating that you will provide "consulting services" is ambiguous. How will you and your client determine whether you have adequately performed, especially if there is a dispute about your performance (because that's when everyone will look to the contract)?

Your perspective of whether a contract is clear versus ambiguous may not match your client's perspective. In addition, what you consider unambiguous, might still be unclear under the law. My local law library has a book entitled, *Words and Phrases*, which contains a collection of definitions and interpretations Virginia courts have adopted during lawsuits where parties to contracts have asked the court to clear up ambiguous contract language. So even if you think you know what a word or phrase in a contract means, courts might have adopted a different definition.

Ambiguous words and phrases in contracts probably won't be enforceable. In addition, if you go to court to ask a judge to interpret ambiguous words and phrases, state law might prohibit the judge from considering conversations or correspondence you and your client had about their meaning. In that instance, you will be stuck with a contract that does not reflect the deal you thought you struck.

Capturing understandings in writing can be difficult. You may believe your client and you "know what you mean," but when a dispute arises, the contract language will be scrutinized and picked apart to support each side's position. A lawyer can review the contract to identify and correct ambiguous words and phrases to help reduce this risk.

Undefined Words

Poorly drafted contracts often include words they fail to define. Undefined words are another form of ambiguity. For example, the contract may refer to the "services" or the "deliverables," but fail to define what those terms mean.

Failing to define keywords used in the contract opens the door to additional ambiguity in the contract.

This problem can be cured by including definitions in the contract for keywords. A lawyer can pick out the undefined keywords and draft definitions for them. Doing so will strengthen the enforceability of the contract, and help avoid disputes (or resolve them quickly by referring to clear contract language).

Agreements to Agree

Clients and gig economy businesses often have difficulty agreeing on all the terms of a project upfront. One way they try to move forward without resolving an issue is to put language in the contract indicating that they will agree upon a resolution in the future. For example, if a gig economy worker will provide consulting services to the client, but the parties cannot agree on the scope of those services, they might put a provision in the contract to indicate that the parties will determine the scope of those services at a later date after the contract has been signed. A common way this occurs is to include a "TBD" or "to be determined" phrase in the contract. This is an agreement to agree.

Agreements to agree are unenforceable in Virginia, and maybe in your state, too. This means putting an agreement to agree provision in a contract is equivalent to leaving that provision out of the contract. A Virginia court will not force one party to agree with another party because the contract lacks details about what the agreement should be. In my example above, for instance, how would a court force one party to agree with the other party on the scope of the consulting services when the parties have provided no details about those services in the contract?

A lawyer can identify agreements to agree and correct them. Of course, one way to correct them is to get the parties to agree on the terms while drafting the contract. Another way is to draft into the contract a method for making the decision later, such as a process for determining the scope of the services after the contract has been signed. As a last resort, you might consider imposing upon each party a contractual obligation to negotiate in good faith for a limited period of time and then have the contract indicate what will happen if the parties cannot come to an agreement by the end of that time period.

Verbal Agreements Not in the Contract

Clients and gig economy workers often attempt to cure any ambiguity in the contract by referring to verbal agreements they made during negotiations. Unfortunately, verbal agreements not put into the written contract probably become unenforceable once the contract is signed. And, as explained above, a court may not consider those verbal agreements as evidence if the parties ask the court to interpret and enforce the written contract.

An example of an unenforceable verbal agreement is a promise by the client that it will engage the gig economy worker for a future project. If the written contract fails to include that promise, then the promise is unenforceable.

This means you will not be able to challenge the client if it awards the future gig to another independent contractor.

A well-drafted contract will contain a "merger clause." This paragraph usually is entitled, "Entire Agreement," and is found near the end of the contract in what people often refer to as the "boilerplate" (more on that below). The merger clause indicates that the written contract contains the entire agreement, and supersedes all verbal agreements and promises the parties made before the contract was signed. The merger clause strengthens the concept that verbal agreements not contained in the contract are unenforceable.

Tell your lawyer everything about the deal you have negotiated with the client so your lawyer can ensure all verbal agreements have been properly memorialized in the written contract. Review the draft contract, as well, to determine whether the verbal agreements have been included. Once you sign the contract, you will not get another chance to incorporate verbal agreements into the contract, unless the client will agree to a written amendment.

Making sure your contract is clear and enforceable will protect you against risks you did not agree to assume. It also will strengthen the enforceability of the contract. If a dispute arises, a clear and enforceable contract will help you resolve the dispute because you will be able to rely on the contract language to tell you who is responsible for what.

WHAT SHOULD YOUR CONTRACT INCLUDE?

Your industry, services offering, and typical clients determine what your template client contract should include. Because I cannot predict those circumstances for every reader of this book, I cannot determine exactly what your particular template client contract will look like. What follows is a description of provisions customarily found in contracts for delivering consulting services or freelance services. Each heading corresponds with the title of a similar heading in those contracts. I also explain how a client might want certain provisions to be drafted to favor it and what is customary and reasonable.

The Parties

The contract must identify the parties who are making the agreement. This might seem obvious to you, but I review many gig economy contracts where the parties are not properly identified. For example, if you are a consultant and have formed an LLC through which you provide your consulting services, you should not be a party to the contract, your LLC should. If you are personally identified as a party to the contract, you will be personally liable for all contractual obligations. It will look like you are a sole proprietorship. You will have ignored your LLC and some of the purposes for which it was created. There will be no protective barrier between your business liabilities and your personal assets.

Your LLC should be identified by its full and correct name to avoid any confusion or ambiguity. A client recently told me its company was named "Pulmonary Wellness

Associates," but when I researched my state's online database of entities, I discovered it was named "Pulmonary Wellness Services," so we corrected the name in the contract before it was signed. That might seem like a minor detail, but it cleared up a potential ambiguity in the contract.

Also, use whatever entity designation you have chosen when forming your entity (e.g., "LLC," "LC," "Inc.") to clearly show that your client is contracting with a legal entity, not a person.

Make sure your client follows these same guidelines.

The Preamble or Purpose Clause

Lawyers have a tradition of drafting a preamble to contracts. These paragraphs typically appear at the beginning of the contract and start with a "Whereas." The objective is to provide some background on the parties and the deal—a quick roadmap about how the parties got to the point of making the contract and what their objectives are.

I think "Whereas" clauses are a turn-off. My view is that they trigger a negative reaction from non-lawyers because they smack the reader with legalese and formality at the very beginning of the contract.

A preamble is not required or necessary, and, I understand that in some circumstances, the details in the preamble might not even be considered an enforceable part of the contract. But the idea of providing some background and explaining the parties' objectives for making the contract is good. My practice is not to use a preamble or "Whereas" clauses, but instead to draft a "Purpose" provision as the first paragraph of the contract. By including it as a provision in the contract, I also increase its enforceability.

Services

This is what the client is engaging you to do. Include a provision that describes the services you will perform with specificity. If the description of the services is going to be lengthy, you might consider defining and describing the services in an exhibit attached to the contract.

If you provided your client with a proposal to win the project, you might be tempted to attach the proposal to the contract as an exhibit to incorporate into the contract everything contained in the proposal. Be careful with that idea. You don't want to create a situation where the proposal contradicts or is inconsistent with your contract. Puffing language used in the proposal for marketing purposes might inadvertently create promises, representations, or warranties you didn't intend. Instead of attaching the entire proposal to the contract, attach only relevant excerpts, such as the scope of services description.

Your performance will be measured against the services described in your contract. In some instances, you might describe what you won't do—i.e., what is outside the scope of your services—if you are concerned the client might not understand the scope of your services.

Specifications; Deliverables; Testing

Specifications create a standard against which your services and deliverables can be measured. For example, if your client engages you to build a website, the contract should describe important design and functional features you must build into the website. If your client engages you to build a mobile software application, the contract should specify the app's functionality requirements. If your client engages you to create a training program for its employees, then the contract should indicate what the client wants in that program. The idea behind including specifications is to help you and your client determine how you are performing, and whether the client is getting what they expect. Specifications also provide an objective measure for evaluating your performance, rather than giving your client the opportunity to reject your performance or deliverables because it is not "satisfied"—an extremely subjective measure.

If you and your client are unable to determine the specifications before signing your contract, the contract should describe the process you and your client will use to develop the specifications. The contract should also describe what will happen if you and your client cannot agree on the specifications after following that process.

Your contract also needs to describe the work product you will deliver to your client. That work product typically is referred to as a "deliverable." For example, if your client engages you to develop a high altitude search-and-rescue training program for emergency responders, the deliverables might include a written guide for the instructor, presentation slides, and a student handbook. If you are engaged to film, direct, and edit a promotional video for your client's website, the deliverable could be the raw video footage and final edit of the video. Whatever your client is buying from you should be described as a deliverable in your contract.

The specifications can include a timeline or deadlines for performing services and delivering work product.

Consider including a trial or testing period in your contract depending on the nature of your deliverables. This gives your client the right to test or try out your deliverables for a short period, to identify any aspects of the deliverables that don't meet the specifications, and to give you an opportunity to fix the identified issues. For example, if you are building a software application based on mutually developed specifications, you might give your client the right to run the application in its business setting for a short period to determine if it meets the specifications. Be careful how you draft the testing provision, however, because you don't want to inadvertently create a never-ending testing loop, especially if some of your fees won't be paid until after a successful test. Limit the number of rounds of testing and indicate what happens if you get to the end of those rounds without the deliverables meeting the specifications.

The specifications, deliverables, and testing provisions are some of the most important aspects of your contract. They likely will change from client to client and project to project. Spend a significant amount of time developing these provisions to decrease your risk of a dispute with your client.

The specifications, deliverables, and testing provisions might be so extensive they are better suited to be included in an exhibit attached to the contract, rather than in the body of the contract.

Change Orders

What happens if shortly after you have started your client's project, you discover the project will take more work than either your client or you expected? This frequently happens in the construction industry, and they have developed a process for handling that issue. If a kitchen remodeler quotes a price for installing new kitchen cabinets, then discovers during the process of hanging the cabinets that the studs in the wall have been destroyed by termites, making it impossible to hang the cabinets, the contractor can present the homeowner with a written change order indicating the additional work that will need to be done to replace the studs and the estimated cost of that work. The homeowner then has the option of accepting the change order (which acts as an amendment to the contract) or rejecting the change order and terminating the contract.

You may also be building something for your client, like a website, software application, or compliance program. If you believe you might discover circumstances during the project that might require a change in the scope of your work or deliverables, that increase your fees, or change your timeline, include a change order provision in your contract. That provision should describe the process for submitting a change order, and the rights your client will have to either accept and pay more, or terminate the contract.

Client Responsibilities

If the nature of your work depends on your client doing something or meeting certain requirements, you need to draft your client's responsibilities into your contract. For example, if you are designing and building a custom software application, include in your contract the hardware and software your client needs to provide at its expense in order to create an environment in which your deliverable will work.

You may need certain of your client's employees to be involved in the project. They may need to provide you with periodic input, to provide ongoing and up-to-date data, or to create certain internal deliverables before you can provide your services or deliverables.

Put in your contract whatever you need from your client to perform your services and provide your deliverables. Be specific. Describe what will happen if your client doesn't meet its responsibilities. For example, you can indicate that you have the right to suspend your work, and ultimately terminate the contract, if your client doesn't do its part within a specified time period.

Term

How long will your contract last? In some instances, it might expire when you finish the project or deliver your work product. In other instances, you might be a long-term consultant providing services on various projects from time-to-time. In either case, indicate in your contract how long it will last.

Termination

You and your client will each have the right to terminate the contract if the other party breaches. Sometimes, however, one or both parties might want the right to terminate the contract in other circumstances. I have seen, for example, a Fortune 500 company ask for the right to terminate my client's consulting contract for convenience (i.e., at any time for any reason or no reason) upon 90 days' written notice to retain some control over how much money the company spends on my client's services. If the company adopts a new budget that doesn't include enough money to pay for my client's services, the company wants the right to terminate the contract, so it is not obligated to pay fees for which it has no budget.

You may want the right to terminate the contract for convenience if you are concerned about getting tied up for too long with a particular client, or on a particular project. You might want to retain some flexibility to terminate a client if another project comes along that will demand more of your time, but also will be more lucrative.

Carefully consider whether to include a right to terminate for convenience in a contract because it brings uncertainty to the relationship. You may not want to give your client the right to terminate for convenience because you might be relying on the future income from the contract to sustain you over a period of time. You don't want to lose that income stream suddenly. Likewise, your client may not want to give you a right to terminate for convenience because it doesn't want a delay in the project caused by the need to find a replacement for you.

Fees; Expenses; Payment Terms

How much will your client pay you for your services? Your deliverables? How will your fees be calculated? When will your fees be paid? Will you require your client to advance a portion of your fees before you begin the project? Address all these items in your contract.

Many gig economy businesses are paid a fee based on an hourly rate. How do you measure your hourly rate, especially when you work only a portion of an hour? By the tenth of an hour or by the quarter of an hour?

Or perhaps you're paid a flat fee.

Sometimes, a client may pay a gig economy business based on performance. For example, one of my clients gets paid a percentage of the increase in revenues her software generates for her clients.

However you will be paid, make sure your contract spells it out in detail.

Also, make sure your contract describes how the client will reimburse you for expenses you incur in connection with the project. If you must travel to work on the project, your client should reimburse you for your travel, lodging, and meal costs. Your client likely will want the contract to include a process for approving those reimbursable expenses before you incur them, and that's reasonable. If your client wants to condition reimbursement of your expenses on your compliance with its internal expense reimbursement policy, you should not agree to that approach until after you have had a chance to review a copy of that policy, and to determine if it is reasonable.

Include payment terms in your contract. Will you provide a monthly invoice to your client? Will your client be required to pay your invoice within a certain time period (e.g., 30 days)? Is your client paying a monthly flat fee, or advance without the need for a monthly invoice? These details need to be in your contract.

Some clients may want language in your contract about paying only "undisputed" fees. I dislike that language because it gives the client a lot of leverage over you in the event it wants to stop paying you based on its subjective, unilateral determination of dissatisfaction. If a client insists on language of this sort, include language that requires immediate payment of undisputed fees and creates a fast process for resolution of disputed fees to avoid a lengthy interruption in your income stream.

Exclusivity

Some clients may want you to work exclusively for them during your contractual relationship. Or a client might want to restrict you from working for its competitors during the project. Think deeply about whether to agree to such restrictions. Can you do so without harming your ability to generate income?

If a client asks for exclusivity and you are reluctant to give it, explain to your client that the confidentiality and work product ownership provisions protect it from your use of its confidential information and that work product for projects with its competitors. Those restrictions result in implied exclusivity, without the need for an express (and perhaps broader) exclusivity provision.

Work Product Ownership

This issue is one of the most heavily negotiated provisions in gig economy contracts. It's often also one of the most misunderstood. I discuss this issue in-depth in Chapter Two.

Many unsophisticated clients believe paying for your services means they have purchased the intellectual property rights to your work product. That belief usually is false.

Sophisticated clients know you usually retain ownership of the intellectual property rights to work product you create, and, therefore, want an extremely broad contract provision transferring all of those ownership rights to them. That approach is usually too broad and asks you to give up too much.

Chapter Two suggests an approach for handling this issue in a way that is reasonable to both your client and you.

Toolkit Ownership

This issue is almost never addressed in gig economy contracts, especially if the client presents its template contract to you.

You bring to the project your expertise and know-how, created before your client engaged you. You also might bring things to the project that you created before your client engaged you, such as software code, graphic designs, workflow designs, questionnaires, and other tools you use to perform your services and create deliverables. I call all this stuff your "toolkit."

Don't inadvertently transfer ownership to your toolkit to your client. That might happen if the work product ownership language is too broad. If you transfer ownership to your toolkit, you technically lose the rights to use your toolkit for yourself or any other clients. That would destroy your gig economy business.

Chapter Two suggests how to handle this issue in your contract.

Confidentiality

Your client will disclose confidential information to you for the project. You also will disclose your confidential information to your client. For example, your toolkit might contain trade secrets that are intertwined into the work product you deliver to your client. Include a provision in your contract that requires you to protect your client's confidential information and requires your client to protect your confidential information. If your client presents you with its template contract, read the confidentiality provision carefully. The confidentiality provision in many client-presented template contracts I review protects only the client. If that is the case, you need to revise that provision to protect you, as well.

Portfolio Use

Consider including a provision in your contract that allows you to use examples of your work product and deliverables in your portfolio if you are in an industry where you get gigs based on your body of prior work. Some clients may be reluctant to give you this right, but you can comfort them by reminding them that you are obligated not to disclose their confidential information. If they are still reluctant, consider whether you can modify the work product or deliverable to remove any information that might indicate your client's identity, goods, or services.

Related to portfolio use is the right to identify your client in your marketing materials. Including a client without its permission raises the risks of ruining your client relationship and getting a reputation for sleazy marketing practices. If you want to identify your client in a list of representative clients on your website or in other marketing materials, include a provision in your contract giving you that right.

Non-Circumvention

You might introduce your client to other individuals, businesses, or opportunities during the project. A non-circumvention provision prohibits your client from going around you. Include a non-circumvention provision in your contract if you want to stay in the middle of the relationships you broker to your client.

For example, if you use subcontractors to help provide services and deliverables, you have the contractual relationship with your subcontractors, but your client might have direct contact with them. You may want to avoid a situation where your client engages your subcontractor directly; you don't want to get cut out of the deal, especially if you are marking up the fees for your subcontractors. A non-circumvention provision can protect your interests in these circumstances.

Warranties; Disclaimers; Remedies

This is another extremely important aspect of your gig economy contract, even though it might not appear so on its face.

Warranties are promises you make to your client about your services and deliverables. Clients rarely make any warranties to gig economy workers, but they usually require the gig economy worker to give warranties to them. Be careful about the warranties you make.

Some common warranties clients want include: (a) that the services are performed in accordance with applicable laws; (b) that the services are performed in a workmanlike manner in accordance with applicable industry standards; (c) that the services are performed in accordance with, and the deliverables meet, the specifications; (d) that the services and deliverables do not infringe on anyone's intellectual property rights; and (e) that you are not restricted or prohibited by another contract from performing the services. These warranties are reasonable if properly worded.

The law also might imply certain warranties, such as the warranty of merchantability and the warranty of fitness for a particular purpose. If you are creating and delivering software or a website, the law might imply certain additional warranties, such as a warranty that the code will not contain any bugs or malicious code and will operate error-free. Research the types of implied warranties that might apply to your services and deliverables, then determine whether you should include language in your contract to disclaim them. Normally, disclaimers of implied warranties are expected and agreed to in a gig economy contract.

Spell out in the contract what will happen if you breach a warranty. For example, if the website you developed does not have the functionality described in the specifications, what will you do? Will you fix it for free within a certain time period? Will you refund money if you cannot fix it within that time period? Will you pay the client's fees and expenses for replacing the website or for another contractor to fix it? Will the client have the right to terminate the contract? I'm not suggesting with this line of questions that these are the remedies you need to put in your contract. Instead, I'm suggesting you need to think deeply about the remedies you will offer and how to describe them in the contract. You don't want to over-promise and create a situation where your remedy breaks your gig economy business financially.

Indemnification

Indemnification is a promise by one party to pay or reimburse the other party for losses, damages, costs, and expenses it suffers as a result of the first party's acts, omissions, or breach of the contract. For example, if you create an online store for your client that has inadequate security protections, and, as a result, your client suffers a security breach where its customers' credit card information is stolen, the customers might sue your client, but the client will, in turn, require you to defend it and pay or reimburse it for any losses.

Clients of gig economy businesses typically require the contractor to indemnify the client for any losses, damages, costs, and expenses suffered as a result of an infringement of someone else's intellectual property rights (e.g., copyright, trade secret, patent, or trademark) by the contractor. That's reasonable because the client typically has no control over that issue.

An indemnification provision also is appropriate if your services or deliverables might cause property damage, personal injury, or death to a client or its employees, other contractors, customers, or the general public.

The scope of an acceptable indemnification provision will depend on what's typical in your industry, the nature and riskiness of your services, and the types of deliverables you will provide.

An indemnification provision can be difficult to understand, so I recommend you have an experienced lawyer review and explain it to you. She also should suggest reasonable changes to that provision to protect your interests, if necessary.

Limitations on Liability

How much potential liability might you encounter by performing services and creating deliverables for a client? That will depend on a number of factors, including the type of industry you're in, the nature of your work, and the type of services you will perform and deliverables you will provide. Analyze these factors to develop a rough estimate of your potential exposure to your client and its end users (e.g., employees or customers).

Including a provision in your contract that limits your potential liability allows you to predict your worst-case scenario in the event a problem arises.

It's customary and reasonable to disclaim all special, consequential, exemplary, and punitive damages. All of these types of damages have specific legal meanings that aren't necessary to explain in this book. Just know you don't want them in your contract, and that any reasonable client will allow you to disclaim them. Sometimes a gig economy contract will go so far to indicate that the gig economy business will not be responsible for certain specific types of losses, such as lost profits or lost data.

It's also customary that the contract not limit liability for intellectual property infringement claims.

Frequently, gig economy workers want a provision that limits the amount of their potential liability exposure to the fees they are paid under the contract. This is called a "cap." Clients might not agree to that limitation, especially if the fees might be relatively low in comparison to a client's perceived damages resulting from your breach of the contract. In that event, offer a liability cap that is a multiple of the fees you are receiving, such as two times that amount (or more, if you want to still try to limit your liability with a client who wants no liability cap).

Insurance

There is no need for you to voluntarily put a provision in your contract requiring you to have insurance, but your client might require you to have it, so be ready for that issue.

If you already have insurance in place, make sure the insurance provision your client wants matches up with the insurance you already have. For example, if the client requests $2,000,000 of liability insurance, and you have a policy with a $1,000,000 limit, ask your client if it will accept your existing limit.

Sometimes a client presents you with a template contract designed to be used with any type of contractor, not just a gig economy worker. That contract might require insurance you don't need, such as workers' compensation insurance or automobile insurance. Or it might require a certain type of liability insurance to cover you while you are at the client's jobsite when you actually will provide services remotely. In those cases, negotiate revisions to the insurance provisions to match the circumstances of your gig economy business and the project.

If your client won't back down from its insurance requirements and you will need to buy new or more insurance, ask the client to pay your premium (or increased premium), or increase your fees to incorporate the new or increased premium. It's a cost of doing business that you didn't originally factor into your fees because you were not aware your client would require the insurance.

Relationship of Parties

This provision is meant to clearly indicate that you are your client's independent contractor and not its employee. It also indicates that you and your client are not entering into a partnership relationship (see Chapter One for an explanation of why partnerships are risky). While this provision alone won't define the nature of the relationship (see above for a discussion of what makes you your client's independent contractor versus an employee), it's customary and expected in a gig economy contract.

Subcontractors

If you think you might use subcontractors to help you fulfill a contract, put a provision in your contract allowing you to do so. Your client might want to have the right to pre-approve your subcontractors or to have you remove them from the project. Your client may also want you to promise that your subcontract will contain the same terms and conditions as your contract with it. That's all reasonable.

On the other hand, your client's template contract might prohibit you from using subcontractors for the project under any circumstances. You will need to negotiate a more reasonable provision (e.g., to include the client controls explained in the prior paragraph), if you need to use subcontractors for the project.

Dispute Resolution

Consider including a provision in your contract about how disputes will be resolved. Not including a dispute resolution provision allows each party to choose how it wants to resolve a dispute, which usually means a lawsuit.

A dispute resolution provision usually is included in a contract to require the parties to use a process other than litigation (called "alternative dispute resolution") to resolve disputes. The conventional wisdom is that alternative dispute resolution favors the party with less money, which probably will be you.

Many times, alternative dispute resolution is a tiered process. For example, requiring first negotiation, then mediation if negotiation fails, then arbitration if mediation fails. Arbitration can be binding or non-binding.

If you decide to include a dispute resolution provision in your contract, make sure it clearly indicates what processes will be used, how to start the process, where you will meet, who will make the decisions, who will pay the expenses of the process (e.g., for the mediator or arbitrator), whether the loser will pay the winner's legal fees, and whether the arbitration is binding.

Equitable Relief

Courts have two types of authority to resolve lawsuits. They can order the loser to pay the winner for its damages, or they can order the loser to do or to stop doing something. For example, if your client doesn't pay you for your services, you can sue the client and get those fees paid if you win. On the other hand, if your client is using your confidential information without your permission, you probably want the court to order your client to stop. A court order to do or not do something is called "equitable relief." Equitable relief is generally available when money damages won't be adequate to resolve the dispute.

It's customary to put an equitable relief provision in your contract if either party might breach the contract in a way that can't be cured by the payment of money damages. Both your client and you should want this provision in your contract. It should indicate which provisions in the contract qualify for equitable relief.

Boilerplate

The end of the contract will contain a section entitled "Miscellaneous Provisions" or "General Provisions." The provisions in this section are commonly referred to as "boilerplate." You can research why it's called boilerplate, but you don't need to know why for purposes of creating a contract. Some hold the position that these provisions are called "boilerplate" because they cannot be negotiated. That's not true. Others hold the position that the boilerplate provisions do not really impact the deal. That's not true, either.

Provisions commonly found in the boilerplate of a gig economy business's contract include:

Severability

Contract law in your jurisdiction may indicate that if part of the contract is unenforceable, the entire contract is void. The severability provision is included to avoid that risk. It provides that if any portion of the contract is unenforceable, then the remainder of the contract will still be enforceable and read and interpreted as if the unenforceable portion were no longer in the contract. This provision is necessary but typically requires no negotiation.

Entire Agreement or Merger

Neither party wants to risk having the other party claim the contract does not contain all the agreements they made about the project. To prevent that risk, the contract should contain a provision indicating that the contract contains all of the agreements made about the deal. That provision will indicate that the contract supersedes all prior negotiations, offers, verbal representations and warranties, and verbal and written communications that might be construed as agreements (e.g., emails). Lawyers refer to this contract principle as a "merger" of all prior communications into the contract, so the title of this provision may sometimes be or contain the word "Merger." This provision is necessary, but should reflect the reality of the circumstances. For example, if there are other agreements related to the deal, such as a separate Confidentiality Agreement between the client and you, this provision should be changed to refer to that separate agreement and indicate that the contract does not invalidate it, but that the additional contract makes up part of the deal.

Modification or Amendment

Neither party wants to take the risk the other party might claim the contract has been changed without its permission. For example, you do not want to risk your client claiming the amount of your fees was decreased because you sent an email to the client after signing the contract indicating that the project will take longer than originally expected. This provision allows for amendments or modifications to the contract, but only if those changes are in writing and signed by both parties. This provision is necessary but usually does not require any negotiation as long as it prevents either party from unilaterally changing the contract.

Waiver

Neither party wants to take the risk the other party might claim it is no longer obligated to do something required by the contract because the first party did not enforce the contract when the other party breached. For example, if the contract requires the client to pay you on the first day of each month, but the client doesn't pay you until the 20th of the month for three months in a row, the client should not be able to claim that the obligation to pay on the first of the month is now unenforceable just because you did not insist on payment by that date in the prior three months.

In other words, if a party does not enforce one provision of the contract, it does not act as a waiver of that provision relieving the other party from its obligations. This provision is necessary to allow each party the flexibility to determine which obligations to enforce and which to let go, without jeopardizing its right to enforce any provision of the contract (including the one it chose not to enforce at one time) in the future. This provision usually does not require negotiation.

Force Majeure

This is a fancy legal term that refers to factors affecting the performance of the contract that are out of the parties' control, such as bad weather, war, terrorism, disease, strikes, riots, crime, or acts of God. If a party to the contract cannot perform due to a force majeure event, its non-performance is excused and not considered a breach of the contract for as long as that event continues. Note that it is customary that the force majeure provision not apply to the payment of your fees. In other words, the client can't stop paying your fees because of a force majeure event.

Governing Law

This provision chooses which state's (or country's) law will govern the interpretation of the contract and any disputes that might arise in connection with the deal. If you and your client are located in the same state, you should choose that state's law. Sometimes people think they should choose another state's law (e.g., Delaware) to govern the contract because it's trendy or might appear more favorable to a certain party. Virginia courts will not apply the law of a state to which neither party has any relation (e.g., based on the location of the business or where the services are performed), so choosing an unrelated state law is a waste of time.

If you and your client are in different states, the choice of governing law is negotiable. If you cannot agree on which state law to choose, I suggest choosing the state law of the state in which your gig economy business is located. Note, however, many clients (especially large businesses) may insist the contract be governed by the law for the state in which the client is located. That's not a deal breaker. You should be aware that if a dispute arises, however, you will need to engage a lawyer in that state to help you.

If your client is in a different country, choice of law also is negotiable. I recommend you insist your contract be governed by the country and state law where your gig economy business is located. You also might need to include and refer to international treaties or conventions. Dealing with an international client always increases risks because of the difference in laws between countries, the distance, and the costs, expenses, and difficulty associated with trying to enforce a contract in another country.

Venue

Venue refers to the location of a lawsuit. Interestingly, lawsuits about the contract can be brought in the federal or state courts sitting in one state, but require those courts to apply the law of a different state as a result of the state law chosen in the Governing Law provision. Choice of venue is strategic because a party may gain leverage in settlement negotiations if another party needs to travel to a distant location to bring or defend a lawsuit. For example, if your gig economy business is located in Virginia, but the client is located in Florida, bringing a lawsuit in Virginia courts against the client may put the client at a disadvantage because he will have to travel to Virginia to defend the lawsuit.

Venue certainly is negotiable, but it should not be a deal breaker. It seems reasonable that the venue should be where your gig economy business is located, but your client might feel strongly about having the venue at its particular location or where the services are performed.

If you appear to be at an impasse on this issue, consider setting venue in your client's location if you bring a lawsuit against the client, or in your location if the client brings a lawsuit against you. This approach puts the risk of travel on the party bringing the lawsuit. This seems like a fair approach because it requires the party initiating the lawsuit to consider the expenses of bringing it in a distant location, which might aid in motivating the parties to settle out of court.

Assignment or No Assignment

The contract usually will contain a provision prohibiting any transfer of the contract by the gig economy business. The client wants to avoid the risk they might end up having the services performed by a new gig economy worker they don't know and didn't choose. This is reasonable because the client is engaging you for your unique personal services, expertise, reputation, and characteristics. In other words, you are one-of-a-kind, and that's why your client is engaging you.

The client may want the right to transfer your contract, however. For example, it might want the right to assign your contract to a buyer of its business so you will continue to provide your services to the new owner. Or, the client might want the right to transfer your contract to an affiliate or subsidiary. In both instances, the client likely won't agree to condition the transfer on receiving your prior written consent—it won't want to give you a veto right over the transfer.

You and your lawyer will need to decide whether a client's request for the right to transfer the contract, with or without your consent, is reasonable, based on the circumstances of your project.

Successors and Assigns

This provision is included to indicate that if the contract is transferred to a new party, it will be binding and enforceable against that new party. This provision is reasonable, and should not require any negotiation unless your lawyer sees something wrong with the language of the provision.

Notices

Other provisions in the contract might require one party to notify another party for certain reasons, such as disputing a fee or making a claim under the indemnification provision. Each party wants to avoid the risk of a situation where it loses its rights under the contract because it did not provide the other party with proper notice of a claim. Likewise, a party does not want to risk getting into a position where it fails to respond to a claim because it did not receive proper notice. Therefore, the contract will contain a "Notice" provision, indicating acceptable ways to give notice (e.g., by Certified Mail, Return Receipt Requested, overnight delivery that can be tracked, fax), when notice will be deemed received, and to whom notice must be given (including all relevant address and contact information).

Note that email notification typically is not an acceptable form of notice because it is too easy to claim an email was never received, or that it was overlooked in a sea of email. If you want email to be an acceptable form of notice, you should clearly indicate that in this provision, but also include requirements for return receipts or acknowledgements before the email notice is deemed effective.

Headings

Each provision in the contract will have a heading, title, or name. There is a risk that the words in a provision will be inconsistent with the heading, title, or name, and that inconsistency will make the meaning of the provision ambiguous. To avoid that risk, the contract usually contains a provision by which the parties agree that the headings, titles, and names of the contract's provisions will be disregarded when interpreting the contract.

Survival

A contract ends when it expires or is terminated by a party. As a result, any promises made in the contract for things that might occur after the contract has expired or been terminated (e.g., confidentiality or indemnification) will also be terminated. That's bad for both parties because most contracts provide for some post-termination promises that flow to each party. To avoid the risk of terminating those promises, the contract should contain a survival provision that provides that the expiration or termination of the contract will not terminate certain provisions of the contract. That provision should identify representations, warranties, and other promises and obligations that will survive the expiration or termination of the contract. Both parties should want this provision, but your lawyer should look closely at its language to ensure it handles the risk properly.

Further Assurances

You might discover after signing the contract that you need a particular document drafted or signed in connection with the project. For example, if you are creating a website for your client and you register the domain in your name, when your client discovers this fact after the contract has been signed, they will want you to work through an online process to transfer the domain name. A good contract will contain a catch-all provision in the boilerplate by which both parties agree to do additional things to satisfy the intent of the contract. This provision should require additional action only upon the reasonable request of the other party, and if the other party pays the costs and expenses for the requested party's actions.

Third-Party Beneficiaries

When you see a provision in the contract with this heading, understand that it is there to prevent people who are not part of the deal from claiming they somehow should benefit from the deal. A good example of this would be one of your creditors requesting your client to pay your fees directly to it to satisfy your debt. This provision is an attempt to prevent that situation.

Attorney's Fees

An attorney's fees provision can accomplish two objectives. First, it should indicate that each party will be responsible for paying its own costs and expenses (including lawyer's fees) for negotiating, drafting, and signing the contract. Second, it should indicate that if one party brings a claim against the other, the loser will pay the winner's reasonable lawyer's fees.

In the American legal system, each party is required to pay its own lawyer's fees in a dispute (e.g., arbitration or lawsuit), even if it wins, unless a statute or contract shifts that responsibility to the loser. No statute likely exists to shift lawyer's fees in a dispute involving the contract between your client and you. Therefore, you should strongly consider putting an attorney's fees provision in your contract.

Having an attorney's fees provision in your contract can motivate people to settle disputes without going to court because it causes people to second-guess the costs and risks of suing the other party. An attorney's fees provision tends to level the playing field if one party has more money than the other party, because it may keep the monied party from using a lawsuit for a weak claim as a way to run up the other party's lawyer's fees to pressure them to settle.

Sometimes, the attorney's fees provisions are separated into two provisions in the contract—one to accomplish the first objective, and the other to accomplish the second objective. That should not matter to you. What should matter is that this risk is addressed.

Sometimes, clients try to impose a unilateral obligation on a gig economy business to pay the client's lawyer's fees if the gig economy business loses a lawsuit (whether brought by the client or the gig economy business). Or you might try to impose that unilateral obligation on a client. In either case, it is reasonable for either party to ask that the obligation be imposed on both parties, rather than on just one.

If you want the attorney's fees provision to apply to different types of disputes, such as arbitration and settlements, you need to make sure the provision clearly says so, otherwise, it probably will not apply in those situations. The contract should clearly give an arbitrator the right to award lawyer's fees to the winner.

Finally, don't give your client a blank check for lawyer's fees. You do not want to create the risk of your client engaging the most expensive lawyer in town for the dispute, and you becoming responsible for paying those lawyer's fees in the event you lose. Therefore, any reference to lawyer's fees, costs, and expenses, should indicate that a party will be responsible for them only if they are "reasonable."

Counterparts

In the past, contract signings were more formal, and lawyers asked that each party sign the same copy of the contract. As business and technology have evolved, clients and contractors frequently do not sit at the same table for a contract signing (or even in the same city, state, or country), or sign the same copy of the contract. Instead, they each have separate copies of the contract they sign at their respective location. These separate copies are referred to as "counterparts." Signing counterparts results in signature pages for the contract containing only one party's signature—i.e., a signature page with only the client's signature and a signature page with only your signature. The contract should have a provision that provides for this practice and indicates that the aggregate of all the signature pages will make up one enforceable contract.

Independent Legal Counsel

This provision asks each party to acknowledge that it was represented by its own lawyer, or if it was not represented, that it had the right to be represented and chose not to be. This provision is especially important if you are dealing with a client who decides it does not want to use a lawyer for the contract (usually to save on costs). In that situation, you do not want the client to come back after the contract was signed and claim you took advantage of them. You do not want to risk the possibility that an unrepresented client could undo the deal. This provision is designed to prevent that risk.

Signature Block

The group of signatures at the end of the contract is referred to as the "signature block." Make sure the right people are signing the contract. If you don't have the correct people signing the contract, you risk not being able to enforce the contract against your client.

If your client is an LLC or corporation, but the signature block requires only the owner to sign in his personal capacity, then the entity will not be obligated to perform (e.g., pay your fees) under the contract. Likewise, if the contract contains promises and obligations that the founder of your client is to perform, such as a personal guaranty of the payment of your fees, the founder will not be obligated to perform if he has not signed the contract in his individual capacity.

Pay attention to see that the signature block includes the correct parties. Each person signing should indicate his or her capacity and authority for signing. For example, if your client is a corporation, the contract should require that the person signing on behalf of the corporation indicate his or her corporate title (e.g., President or Vice President). This seems like an inconsequential issue but could put a huge risk on you if the contract is not signed by the right people with the proper authority to bind your client.

WHERE DO YOU GET YOUR CONTRACT?

You can find many sources for sample contracts. A simple internet search (e.g., for "consulting agreement") will result in a long list of free examples you can review. Online companies also sell template documents. In addition, online document assembly services create agreements by having you fill in minimal information about the contract (e.g., the parties' names and the date when services will begin) and asking you basic questions about your agreement. If a business similar to yours posts its agreement on its website (e.g., as terms and conditions), that also might be a source.

But how will you know which agreement to use, or whether a template you purchase online fits your business, your clients, and your deal? Unless you are a lawyer, it's your best guess. Unfortunately, I have many clients who made that guess without understanding how the presence or lack of certain provisions in the form agreement might harm them.

I have had clients who think contract drafting is easy, and they draft their own contracts from scratch. I usually review those contracts when a dispute arises. Every time the contract is lacking in a way that harms my client. That's a tough position to be in because it's too late to re-draft or clarify the contract. You will live and die by what you signed.

Why would you take that risk? To save some money on lawyer's fees? Think of the legal fees you spend on a well-drafted contract as an investment in your business that will pay dividends when a dispute arises. It's typically much less expensive to pay the legal fees for the preparation or review of a contract than it is to pay the lawyer's fees for a dispute involving a poorly written contract.

Research examples of contracts, pick a few you like, and circle provisions you think will be good for you. That exercise will trigger thoughts and provide a starting point for a contract. Then, hire a lawyer to finish the job. She will appreciate your input because it will help her decide how to proceed. Your lawyer will also help draft for clarity and enforceability.

USE A WRITTEN CONTRACT WITH SUBCONTRACTORS.

These same contracting principles apply to your engagement of subcontractors to help with your clients' projects. You need a written subcontract with each subcontractor.

Make sure each subcontract matches up to the terms of the contract you have with the specific client on whose project your subcontractor will work. If your contract with your client has a confidentiality provision in it, make sure the subcontract binds your subcontractor to that same degree of confidentiality. If your contract with your client transfers ownership of your deliverables to the client, make sure your subcontract requires your subcontractor to transfer ownership of its work product on the project to your company so you can pass ownership through to your client. Failing to mirror or match up the terms and conditions of a subcontractor agreement with the terms and conditions of your client agreement can result in some significant problems you will end up paying for because you didn't pay attention to those issues when engaging your subcontractor.

4

CLIENT DISPUTES

YOU WILL HAVE DISAGREEMENTS AND disputes
with some of your clients. In my experience, most disputes between a gig economy business and its clients center
around payment of fees, delays in performing services, or
dissatisfaction with the quality of the services or deliverables. Prepare yourself now, so you have a strategy in place
for resolving those disputes.

Scott owns a gig economy business that designs and
installs home offices for companies that have large remote
workforces. His business is an authorized dealer of the furniture he recommends in his designs. Scott's business did
a project for a large company that resulted in a six-figure
invoice. Scott has a practice of requiring each client to
pay 50% of the total invoice before beginning the project,
which his client did in this instance. The invoice included
purchase prices for furniture and the fees for design and
installation. Scott's client wasn't satisfied with some of the

furniture. Scott worked with the manufacturer to replace it. He also wrote off the fees for the installation services associated with the unsatisfactory furniture. Scott issued a revised invoice for the balance of the purchase prices and fees. His client didn't pay. What can Scott do to get paid?

Connie owns a gig economy business that provides practice management services to dental practices. Her business entered into a consulting contract with a large dental practice. She provided services for over a year. Connie tried to issue monthly invoices but sometimes didn't issue invoices for six to eight weeks after services were performed. At first, the dental practice paid each invoice in full, but starting in the seventh month of the engagement, the dental practice stopped paying. Eventually, Connie stopped providing services because the invoices weren't paid. The dental practice owed her fees in the mid-six figures. Shortly after Connie stopped providing services, her client sent a letter to her indicating it would pay only a small portion of the past due fees, because the client claimed it was dissatisfied with the quality of Connie's services. What can Connie do to get paid?

WHAT CAN I DO TO PREPARE FOR RESOLVING CLIENT DISPUTES?

Adopt preventative practices to help resolve unforeseen future disputes.

Research your potential clients. It probably would be inappropriate and uncustomary to subject a potential client to a credit or background check, but there are other, less intrusive ways to collect information to help you evaluate a potential client. Search the internet for your potential clients. Review their website if they have one. Look for any online reviews or complaints about the potential client. Check the Better Business Bureau's website for any information. When you get the potential client's address, check Google Maps to see the location and quality of their office space. If the potential client is transferring its business to you from a competitor, gently ask your client why they are making that change. Depending on your industry, consider speaking to colleagues for general information about the potential client.

Draft specific provisions into your template client contract to create incentives for your clients to settle disputes quickly. For example, clearly indicate that you have the right to suspend work on a project for non-payment.

Include an attorney's fees provision in your contract that requires the loser to pay the winner's reasonable lawyer's fees (see Chapter Three). Such a provision will cause your client to consider the risk of having to pay your lawyer's fees as a significant factor in evaluating whether to settle a dispute.

Include a provision allowing you to charge interest on past due fees. You can use the write-off of that interest as a negotiation tool in a fee dispute.

Include a provision requiring mediation within a short period of time after a dispute arises.

Limit and be very specific about the promises you are making about the quality and timing of your services. See the suggestions in Chapter Three about representations, warranties, and disclaimers.

Use payment and collection practices that don't allow a client to avoid or draw out payment. Some gig economy businesses require payment of a portion or all of the project fees in advance before work starts. Others require a minimum monthly payment due at the beginning of each month, which is then trued up at the end of the month with either a credit or debit.

I have observed that clients will pay faster if you make the payment process easier. If you are able to email digital invoices to your clients along with a link to allow them to pay by credit card or bank transfer, then they might pay quicker. Or, if your website contains a feature that allows clients to pay online using a credit card or some other means, your clients might pay faster.

Adopt a process for communicating with your clients when payment is past due. If payment is due within 30 days of an invoice, send the client a soft email reminder on the 31st day. If payment is not received by the 45th day, then send an email with a revised invoice including interest on the past due amount. If payment is not received by the 60th day, then send an email indicating that you will sue to collect past due fees if not paid by the 90th day. Consider using phone calls and texts in lieu of emails to deliver these notices.

In the above example of Scott's design business, he used a combination of most of these techniques. He obtained 50% of the fees in advance, and he included interest and lawyer's fees provisions in the terms and conditions of the template purchase order the client signed. His company also sent reminders of past due fees on a regular basis. Then he sued his client for the past due fees, interest, and lawyer's fees when it still did not pay. The lawsuit prompted his client to pay the balance of the invoice before the trial.

WHAT DO I DO IF MY CLIENT IS UNHAPPY WITH ME?

In the example above about Connie's business, her client indicated it would pay only a significantly reduced amount of her fees because it claimed she had not adequately performed. When Connie came to me for help, the first thing I did was review the contract with her client to determine what promises she made about the quality of her services. I discovered that Connie's promises were limited and specific. I then interviewed Connie and reviewed a portion of her work to determine whether she had kept her promises. After concluding Connie had kept her promises, I used my research and factual information to negotiate a settlement to the fee dispute, which was paid within weeks.

If a client becomes unhappy with your services or work product, ask them a lot of questions as soon as possible about their dissatisfaction. Don't just ask them why, but also ask them when the issue arose, how it arose, and what they want to happen to resolve it. You need as much information as you can reasonably get about their dissatisfaction to help you evaluate how to respond to, and, if necessary, resolve, the dispute.

Next, review your contract. What promises did you make? What limitations did you impose on your promises? What remedies did you agree to if you broke a promise?

Evaluate your performance from your perspective in light of the contractual promises to determine whether your client's complaint has merit.

If your client's position has merit because you made a promise and broke it, then work with your client to implement the remedy required by your contract. If the contract does not include a specified remedy, then negotiate with your client about what it wants to happen next. But don't give your client anything you haven't agreed to in your contract. For example, if you capped your total liability under the contract to the amount of fees paid by the client, then don't agree to pay more.

If you don't believe your client's position has merit, then communicate your position by citing contractual provisions and explaining underlying facts. Of course, this approach is based solely on legal positions, not necessarily on factors affecting the client relationship. If a long-standing client who pays on time and provides recurring projects to your business is unhappy, you might consider complying with their demands or negotiating a compromise to preserve the client relationship, despite what the contract says, and what your legal rights are.

Note that some clients might use dissatisfaction with your services or work product as a pretext for not paying your fees, asking for a discount or refund, or terminating the contract. If the contract does not allow the client to terminate for convenience (i.e., at any time for any reason, or no reason) and the client wants to terminate the contract because it has run out of money to pay for your services, the client might conjure up a breach of contract claim based on its alleged dissatisfaction to create a basis for terminating the contract for cause. In this instance, the client likely will not admit to the true reason for its complaint.

There is no magic way to determine whether your client's complaint is legitimate or a pretext for terminating the contract, but researching past communications with your client and gathering intelligence from informal discussions might give you a sense of your client's true underlying motive. You will then need to evaluate and decide whether resolving the dispute in court is worth more than a negotiated settlement.

WHAT DO I DO IF I CAN'T DELIVER? OR, IF I CAN'T DELIVER ON TIME?

Myles owns a gig economy business that developed a software application for use by temporary staffing agencies. The software can be customized in hundreds of different configurations based on a client's input. When Myles licenses the software to a client, he sells them customization and implementation services. Once a client signs a contract,

Myles and the client meet to determine how the client wants the software customized.

Myles' contract indicates that the client has 10 days after customization is complete to test the software. If the client is not satisfied with the performance of the customized software, it can notify Myles' company. Myles' company then has 10 days to reconfigure the software to satisfy the customer. Then the testing, notification, and resolution process starts over again. But the contract does not indicate if and when this process will end.

One of Myles' clients never was satisfied with the customizations after many rounds of testing and attempted fixes. Myles finally acknowledged his company would not be able to meet the client's specifications for the customization. But the contract did not anticipate this circumstance or indicate what the parties would do in this situation.

If Myles' contract with his client had anticipated this risk, it would have contained provisions about what to do to resolve the dispute when it arose. The contract could have provided for a limited number of testing and fix rounds, after which either party could terminate the contract, and the client would be refunded a portion of fees paid.

If you determine you can't deliver the services or work product in accordance with the contract's requirements, or if you determine you won't be able to deliver on time, review the contract to determine if it indicates what should happen in those instances. Then follow the contract's requirements.

If your contract is silent on the issue, you need to approach your client to negotiate a resolution.

In any case, my experience representing gig economy businesses has taught me that early and constant communication with the client will result in better and faster resolutions to these problems. Hiding or avoiding these issues usually results in an escalation that sours the relationship, breeds distrust, incurs more costs, and damages the contractor's reputation.

Of course, the inability to deliver is not just a legal problem; it's a client relationship issue. Consider other non-legal factors that might drive the resolution of these types of disputes to preserve the client relationship or at least maintain and preserve your reputation in the business community.

WHAT DO I DO IF MY CLIENT WANTS A FREE FIX, A REPLACEMENT, OR A REFUND?

Consumer products usually come with a warranty promising a free fix, replacement, or refund if the customer is not satisfied.

Gig economy services and work product customarily have no or very limited warranties, especially if you use a template client contract that includes customary provisions about representations, warranties, and disclaimers (see Chapter Three).

Some clients may unreasonably believe or expect that your gig economy services and deliverables are covered by representations and warranties similar to those for consumer products. In that instance, a client might demand a free fix, replacement, or refund if it believes you have breached your representations and warranties.

When a client complains about the quality of your services or deliverables, both of you need to review the contract to determine (1) the representations and warranties you made, and (2) the remedies you promised if a representation or warranty is breached. Assuming you breached a representation or warranty, what remedy does the contract indicate is due the client? If it's a free fix, replacement, or refund, then you both need to follow that requirement.

If the contract does not indicate remedies for a breach of a representation or warranty, the breach is simply a breach of the entire contract. The remedies available to the client are the same ones the law would make available for any other breach of contract. The client could sue you for the damages it suffered as a result of the breach. Damages might include the costs it incurs to buy replacement services or work product. Note, however, that the client probably will not be able to get a court to order you to fix or replace your services or deliverables.

The risks that could arise from your client expecting a free fix, replacement, or refund can be reduced by well-drafted contractual provisions about representations, warranties, and remedies (see Chapter Three).

WHAT DO I DO IF MY CLIENT WON'T PAY?

Non-payment is the most common dispute I see gig economy businesses have with clients. What can you do if your client doesn't pay after you've exhausted your internal invoicing and collection process?

The most common approach I see from gig economy businesses to resolve this type of dispute is to ask a lawyer to send a demand letter to the delinquent client. Many gig economy businesses believe a client will be more likely to comply with a demand letter from a lawyer. They think a lawyer's letterhead will motivate the client into paying. I thought the same thing when I was a young lawyer.

Scott's design business (described at the beginning of this Chapter) had issues collecting from several clients, not just the one described above. I sent demand letters to all of them. The amounts past due for the other clients, however, were much lower—in the low to mid-four figures—than the past due amount for the client described above. In one instance, the client reported he was unaware of the invoice (even though Scott had sent it multiple times) and asked for a new copy. Once a copy of the invoice was provided, the client promptly paid without any more effort from me, so my letter resulted in a good resolution for my client.

Another client never responded to my letter. Instead, it contacted Scott's business directly and set up a payment plan. Again, the demand letter resulted in a good resolution for my client.

Of course, the demand letter to the client owing Scott's business the largest amount of money was completely ignored—no phone calls, no email, and no letter responding to the demand.

In most instances, however, I have found that a demand letter from a lawyer doesn't result in payment. I can't deduce why this is so, but I have guesses. Perhaps it's because the client has no money and has a number of creditors trying to collect. In that instance, the client may be receiving lots of demand letters and ignoring all of them. Other clients may not feel a letter from a lawyer is much of a threat. Still others may not respond or pay because they are calling the gig economy business's bluff, betting that the gig economy business won't follow through and sue for the past due amount.

A lawyer's demand letter, by itself, is not a strong tool for resolution. When a gig economy business asks me to send a demand letter for past due fees, I ask whether the business is willing to file a lawsuit to collect those fees if its client does not respond or pay within a short period of time. My clients often are surprised at that question because they don't understand its purpose. My view is that a demand letter is a threat. That threat has no weight if my client isn't already resolved to sue to collect if the demand letter is ignored. Therefore, if the client isn't fully committed to suing the client, I will not proceed with sending the demand letter because my client's weakness will soon be apparent when my client doesn't follow through with the threat. That weakness will damage the gig economy business's credibility, and, as a result, its ability to collect from its delinquent client.

The bottom line is that you need to be prepared to sue your client to collect past due fees unless you have a good reason not to. I can think of four good reasons not to sue to collect fees.

First, in the event your business has malpractice or errors and omissions insurance, your insurer might prohibit you from suing to collect fees as a way to prevent counter-suits for malpractice. Even if your insurer doesn't have such a policy, you might not want to file a lawsuit if you think it might expose you to a counterclaim for malpractice, negligence, or breach of contract.

Second, your contract with your client might prohibit a lawsuit. Instead, it might require mediation or binding arbitration to resolve a fee dispute.

Third, the economics of the dispute might not justify a lawsuit. For example, if your client owes you $500, but a lawyer charges a $750 flat fee for a collection matter, and there is no provision for the award of lawyer's fees in your contract, it doesn't make sense to file that lawsuit. It's cheaper to write off the past due fees as a loss than to collect it. You may have heard that collection lawyer's take a contingency fee (a percentage of the amount collected) rather than charging an hourly fee or a flat fee. While this is generally true, rarely will a lawyer agree to take a case on a contingency fee basis if the amount to be collected is low. In other words, a lawyer will not agree to take on a matter to collect $500 for 25% of the amount collected.

Fourth, you may have a non-legal reason for not collecting. As discussed before, you might want to preserve a client relationship. Or, you might want to preserve your reputation in the business community. Few gig economy businesses want to be known as "sue-happy," because that reputation might scare off potential clients.

WHAT DO I DO IF MY CLIENT SUES ME?

This is not the time to demonstrate your ability to do it yourself. Consult and engage a qualified lawyer as soon as possible. Lawsuits are too risky to handle *pro se* (without a lawyer).

Lawsuits require not only knowledge of the applicable law, but also knowledge of the court rules and procedures, such as filing procedures and deadlines. If you fail to follow the applicable court rules and procedures, you might lose the lawsuit and have a judgment entered against you. Sure, you can appeal if you lose, but engaging a lawyer for the appeal will cost more than engaging a lawyer for the trial.

Check the statutes for the state in which your LLC or corporation was formed. Some states prohibit an LLC or corporation from representing itself in court. This means that an LLC or corporation that is sued must engage a lawyer to represent it in the lawsuit.

5

GETTING LEGAL HELP

CAROL WAS AN EXECUTIVE AT a large video production company. The company was acquired, and Carol was downsized shortly thereafter. She was unable to find suitable work, so she decided to launch her own video production company. She used an online document assembly service to form a limited liability company. When Carol received the legal documents, she arranged a consultation with me.

Carol had a lot of questions about the LLC documents, which I was able to answer during our consultation. She also asked whether I could identify any other legal issues related to starting her gig economy business. Later, Carol came directly to me for help in starting a separate LLC to purchase an existing videography company. I also reviewed and revised the legal documents for the purchase of that gig economy business.

WHY DO YOU NEED LEGAL HELP TO START YOUR GIG ECONOMY BUSINESS?

Why do you need a dentist to work on your teeth? Why do you need a doctor to diagnose and treat illnesses? Why do you need an architect to design an office building?

Why would a client hire your gig economy business, rather than doing it themselves? Experience, expertise, and efficiency.

You engage a professional because they have been educated and licensed, and have experience with the complex issues you face. You engage them to do something for you that you should not do for yourself because of the significant risks involved. It makes better economic sense to pay a professional to do it right.

Here's how a lawyer can help you with the legal issues associated with starting and running your gig economy business:

- A lawyer will help you determine whether there are any restrictions on starting your gig economy business. She will review employment agreements and employment handbooks and interpret them based on the lawyer's understanding of applicable law to determine whether they impose any enforceable restrictions on your ability to start and run your gig economy business.
- A lawyer will answer your legal questions about starting a gig economy business.

- She will help you determine whether to start an LLC or an S corporation.
- She will draft and file the Articles of Organization or Articles of Incorporation to start the legal entity for your gig economy business.
- She will apply her experience to your circumstances to provide guidance on how to structure the setup of your new gig economy business.
- She will draft the legal documents necessary to complete the formation of your LLC or S corporation.
- A lawyer will answer questions you have about your LLC or S corporation legal documents.
- She will help you identify your toolkit and suggest ways to protect it.
- A lawyer will draft your template client contract.
- She will review changes to your contract requested by your prospective clients and advise you on how to respond to those requests.
- She will help you develop a strategy for negotiating a contract with a prospective client.
- A lawyer will review a contract presented to you by a client and suggest revisions to protect your interests.
- She will identify intellectual property and advise you on how to protect and transfer it.
- She will help you resolve disputes with clients through negotiation based on the terms and conditions of your client contracts.
- A lawyer can help you collect past due fees.

- She can file lawsuits against your clients and defend lawsuits filed by your clients against you.
- Your lawyer can filter legal issues to help you understand which issues and risks require more attention and which ones require less.

When you engage a lawyer, you buy her legal knowledge about starting and running gig economy businesses, her legal experience representing gig economy businesses, her intellectual ability to apply the law to your circumstances, her legal counsel, and her legal skills (e.g., contract drafting skills and negotiation skills).

Why wouldn't you engage a lawyer to help you start and run your gig economy business?

WHAT TYPE OF LEGAL HELP DO YOU NEED?

Gig economy businesses face a mixture of corporate, contract, and intellectual property law risks. Look for a lawyer who has legal knowledge and experience addressing these risks in the gig economy business setting.

A trial lawyer, family lawyer, traffic defense lawyer, personal injury lawyer, general practice lawyer, real estate lawyer, estate lawyer, or criminal defense lawyer likely does not have the legal knowledge or experience with gig economy businesses you will need. Therefore, I suggest ruling those types of lawyers out of your search from the beginning.

Many corporate or business lawyers have the skill set to help you. They are well-versed and experienced in helping clients choose and set up the legal entity for a new business. They also have knowledge and experience drafting and reviewing contracts.

You also will need a lawyer with intellectual property law experience. Many corporate and business lawyers may not have that knowledge and experience and may suggest you engage an additional lawyer for those legal issues. You can decide whether you want two lawyers working on your project. Note, however, that some corporate and business lawyers have intellectual property law knowledge and experience (and some intellectual property law lawyers have general business and contract law experience).

Larger law firms may have a team of lawyers (e.g., a separate business lawyer, contract lawyer, and intellectual property lawyer) who can represent you in each legal area. While using such a law firm might appear advantageous, realize your legal fees will be higher than if you use one lawyer at a smaller law firm who can handle all your gig economy business legal issues.

HOW DO YOU FIND A LAWYER TO HELP YOU?

An internet search for a "gig economy lawyer" will yield few results (at least at the time I am writing this book), while a search for a business, corporate, contract, or intellectual property lawyer in your area will result in a long list of suggested lawyers and law firms.

State and local bars may have a lawyer referral service you can use for free or low cost. These referral services probably won't be very helpful in your search because they do not categorize participating lawyers as "gig economy lawyers."

The best way to find a gig economy lawyer is to ask for recommendations from other professionals and colleagues. If you have or are acquainted with an accountant, ask him for a recommendation. Ask your colleagues and even competitors about lawyers they have used or suggest for gig economy business legal services. These requests should help narrow your search.

In the end, you will not be able to select your lawyer until you have a consultation with her where you can ask her questions about her knowledge and experience with gig economy businesses. You also need to meet with lawyers to determine whether your personalities mesh. Consider meeting with a few lawyers to interview them before you decide. If a lawyer does not appear to be a good fit, ask them who they would recommend to help you.

Note that the lawyers you want to interview might not give free initial consultations. Free consultations usually are offered by personal injury, criminal defense, traffic, and divorce lawyers as a marketing tool to entice you into their office for their sales pitch. So, expect to pay a fee for your consultation.

An initial consultation generally is not designed to provide significant legal advice. Don't expect a lawyer to review and advise you on a contract while sitting in an initial consultation. In fact, pressing a lawyer for contract review or other significant legal advice during an initial consultation is unfair to the lawyer and might result in incomplete or poor advice. It's also a turnoff to most lawyers, which might result in them not wanting you as a client. Instead, interview the lawyer and allow her to use that time to interview you and evaluate your startup project.

WHAT ABOUT USING AN INCORPORATION SERVICE FOR STARTING MY ENTITY?

If you search "starting a business," "starting an LLC," or "incorporation" on the internet, you will find many online companies offering legal entity formation services. These incorporation services offer to draft and file the legal document to start your entity with any state of your choice, to draft the legal documents associated with the formation of your legal entity, to obtain the Employer Identification Number from the IRS for your new entity, and to act as your registered agent.

These incorporation services entice you by offering to start your LLC or S corporation for a very low fee (e.g., $125.00).

Beware of the following two drawbacks to using an incorporation service. First, the service won't answer any questions or give you any legal advice. They won't help you choose which entity might be best for the circumstances of your gig economy business. And they won't tailor or customize legal entity documents for you based on your circumstances or objectives.

Second, while these incorporation services portray themselves as a less expensive alternative to a traditional business lawyer, that might not be so. These companies break down the startup services you need into small parts and charge a separate fee for each part. The low fee they quote typically applies only to the service of drafting and filing your Articles of Organization or Articles of Incorporation. But you will need more than that. Incorporation services hope you will engage them because of the low initial fee, and then pay more fees for services you later realize you need. By the time you select all the services you need to start up your legal entity appropriately, your fees likely will approximate the legal fees you might pay a business lawyer. Lawyers at small law firms will provide more service (e.g., you can ask the lawyer questions and get customized legal advice for your project) for a similar fee.

WHAT ABOUT USING A DOCUMENT ASSEMBLY SERVICE FOR CREATING MY TEMPLATE CLIENT CONTRACT?

There are many websites that sell templates of legal documents or provide document assembly services based on your answers to basic questions. You can buy these templates for very low prices. You also may find websites with free collections of sample legal documents. Use these services at your peril. My experience with gig economy businesses who have purchased or downloaded free templates online is that the templates either leave out significant provisions needed for my client's type of gig economy business or contain legal provisions that have a negative impact on my client.

Templates of legal documents offered on each website were one time drafted to address a client's particular needs based on the facts and circumstances of a distinct project. Likewise, legal documents assembled in response to answers to basic questions is a one-size-fits-all approach to addressing unique legal issues raised by your gig economy business or project. Without the input of a gig economy business lawyer, how will you know if a purchased template fits the particular needs and circumstances of your gig economy business or a specific project?

Some of these services attempt to address concerns about tailoring or customizing their products to fit your gig economy business or project by acting as referral sources to local lawyers who have signed up to take on legal projects at a reduced rate. That reduced rate might apply, however, only to a basic consultation. Regular legal rates typically apply for any additional legal work.

As with incorporation services, document assembly services or template websites usually lure you in with a small initial fee, then upsell you to obtain more fees for services you would need and could obtain from a local lawyer for a similar fee.

WHAT MIGHT YOU EXPECT TO PAY A
LAWYER TO FORM YOUR ENTITY?

Most gig economy businesses are started on a shoe-string for a variety of reasons. Paying a lawyer to help you, however, is a sound investment in your business. Legal fees should be part of your startup budget to reduce legal risks and protect your interests.

Most lawyers charge for their services based on the amount of time they spend working on the project. They charge for time spent in consultations with you, researching the law, drafting legal documents, drafting correspondence, negotiating with adverse parties, and responding to your phone calls, emails, and text messages. In my city at the time I am writing this book, you will find business lawyers who charge anywhere from $250 to $500 or more per hour for their legal services. Hourly rates usually correlate to the size of the law firm (a larger law firm means higher rates) and the number of years a lawyer has been in practice (the longer in practice, the higher the rate).

Lawyers also charge flat fees for certain types of legal services. A flat fee does not increase or decrease based on the amount of time a lawyer spends working on the project. Many business lawyers I know charge a flat fee for starting a legal entity. Those startup services might include an initial consultation, drafting and filing the legal documents to start the entity, drafting and filing the IRS form to obtain the Employer Identification Number, drafting the legal documents to complete the formation of the entity (e.g., an Operating Agreement for an LLC), acting as your entity's registered agent for the first year, and shepherding the legal documents through the process to see that they are all properly signed. In my area at the time I am writing this book, I am aware that lawyers charge anywhere from $600 to $1,200 as a flat fee to start a new entity.

WHAT MIGHT YOU EXPECT TO PAY A LAWYER TO DRAFT YOUR TEMPLATE CLIENT CONTRACT?

I cannot predict what your lawyer will charge for drafting your template client contract. Drafting a template contract does not just consist of writing words. It involves gathering the facts and circumstances of the proposed contractual relationships, conducting legal research, if necessary, about the way to draft contractual provisions to improve enforceability, and researching prior art for starting points to draft contractual provisions. The initial draft should then be sent to you for review, input, and questions before it is finalized and ready for your use.

All that legal work takes time, and the time it will take depends on the type of contract needed, the lawyer's experience with drafting, reviewing, and negotiating similar contracts, the type of client you expect to have, and time to interact with you to refine and finalize the template contract. The legal fees incurred in association with drafting your template client contract will be tied to the amount of time the lawyer needs to accomplish these tasks.

Lawyers typically do not draft contracts from scratch. Most experienced lawyers have a personal library of contracts from prior projects to act as starting points for new projects. Ask your lawyer whether she has a template from which to start your template client contract. Also ask her for an estimate of the time it will take to draft and finalize your template client contract.

Even if a lawyer does not have a form in her library to act as a starting point for your template client contract, she has access to reliable, well-respected resources that include examples of form contracts for many different purposes. Your lawyer may or may not charge you legal fees for her research in connection with finding a starting point from a commercial form library.

Ask the lawyer for an estimate. If a lawyer is reluctant to estimate the fees associated with drafting your template client contract, ask her to give you an estimated range of fees—e.g., "legal fees might be somewhere in the range of $750 to $1,500." Ask if she can predict what might put you at the bottom and top of the range. This input will help you budget for those legal expenses.

Some lawyers might be willing to quote a flat fee for drafting your template client contract. That flat fee likely will have a close relation to the hourly rate you would pay based on the lawyer's estimate of how much time it will take her to draft the template client contract.

Some might agree to a cap on their hourly legal fees. If a lawyer quotes you a range, ask her if she will cap her legal fees at the dollar amount at the top of the range.

Some lawyers have developed alternative billing methods for charging legal fees in connection with drafting a contract. For example, some lawyers charge a per page fee (e.g., $50 per-page) for drafting. That fee includes one round of client-requested revisions. The lawyer then charges an hourly rate for additional rounds of client-requested revisions until the template client contract is finalized and ready for your use.

Regard the legal fees for drafting a good template client contract as an investment in your business. It should pay dividends over time. For example, if you pay your lawyer $1,000 to draft your template client contract and 20 clients sign it, the true cost of your contract is $50 per client, which is easily justified by the fees you will be paid by those clients.

WHAT MIGHT YOU EXPECT TO PAY A LAWYER TO REVIEW A CONTRACT OR REQUESTED CHANGES PRESENTED TO YOU BY A CLIENT?

Expect the legal fees for review services to be less than the legal fees for drafting a contract. Your gig economy business lawyer will need less time to review the client's contract or requested changes to your template client contract for significant risks to your interests, such as language that transfers ownership to your toolkit to the client.

In some instances, your lawyer might need to redraft certain provisions of the client's contract or its requested revisions to your template client contract.

In other instances, there might be multiple rounds of review, negotiation, and revisions to the contract.

The methods for measuring legal fees for contract review and revision are similar to those methods for measuring legal fees for contract drafting. Your lawyer might charge an hourly rate, a flat fee, or a per-page rate. In any case, ask for an estimate, even if stated as a range of fees, to help you budget for these expenses.

6

NEXT STEPS

I'VE GIVEN YOU THE BEST look I can at the legal issues and risks of starting a gig economy business. Hopefully, this book has made you more comfortable with leaping from your current situation into your business.

Finishing this book is the beginning of your gig economy business startup journey. You are armed with enough information to prepare you for tackling most of the legal issues you will encounter along the way.

This book crams a lot of information into a small space. Below are checklists summarizing the information presented in each Chapter. Use these checklists as a roadmap for implementing what you have learned from this book.

CHAPTER ONE - STARTING A GIG ECONOMY BUSINESS:

❏ Check for an employment agreement, employee handbook, or employment policies with your current or past employer to determine whether they contain any restrictions on starting your gig economy business.

❑ Review any employment agreement, employee handbook, or employment policies you find to identify potential restrictions, such as confidentiality, non-solicitation, non-competition, or intellectual property ownership provisions.

❑ Consult a lawyer for advice on whether discovered contractual or policy restrictions might be enforceable.

❑ Regardless of whether any contractual or policy restrictions exist or are enforceable, consult a lawyer to determine whether any applicable laws (e.g., copyright or trade secret laws) might restrict your ability to start your gig economy business.

❑ Stop pursuing your gig economy business if restrictions exist or if the risk of enforcement is too great.

❑ If you decide to move forward, form an LLC unless there is a good reason to use a C corporation or S corporation. Don't remain a sole proprietorship or partnership.

❑ Research the name you want to use for your LLC (or corporation) to see if it is available with your state, and to gain comfort that it won't infringe on another company's name or trademark. Get a lawyer to help you with name clearance if you have questions or need help evaluating the legal risks of certain names.

❑ File Articles of Organization with your state and pay the filing fee to form your LLC. Have a lawyer do this if you have legal questions or aren't comfortable doing it.

❑ Have a lawyer draft an Operating Agreement for the LLC. Have all the owners (members) sign it.

❑ Obtain an EIN for your LLC from the IRS. Have a lawyer help you with this if you have questions or aren't comfortable doing it on your own.

❑ Obtain a business license from your locality or state, if required.

❑ Open a business bank account and deposit each member's capital contribution.

❑ Document any loans the members make to the LLC.

❑ Register your LLC with your state tax department and employment commission or labor department, if required.

❑ Obtain errors and omissions or liability insurance if your business exposes you to potential liability for negligence.

CHAPTER TWO - INTELLECTUAL PROPERTY:

❑ Gain a basic understanding of copyright, trademark, trade secret, and patent law, and how it might relate to your toolkit, services, and deliverables.

❑ Determine what intellectual property your gig economy business owns.

❑ Determine how you will protect your toolkit using applicable intellectual property laws and contractual provisions.

❑ Protect ideas and concepts contained in proposals by having prospective clients sign a confidentiality agreement and using confidentiality and copyright notices in your proposals.

❑ Determine who will own the deliverables and associated intellectual property rights, and clearly draft ownership retentions, licenses, and transfers into the written contract with your client.

❑ Determine whether you want to use the deliverables created for one client for other clients. If so, negotiate this use with your current client, (along with appropriate restrictions to protect your current client) and put it in your written contract (if you are at the beginning of the relationship) or a written amendment to your contract (if this issue comes up after you and your client have signed a written contract).

❑ Determine whether you want to use deliverables created for clients in your portfolio. If so, negotiate this use with your clients (along with appropriate restrictions to protect your clients), and put your agreement in your written contract (if you are at the beginning of the relationship) or a written amendment to that contract (if this issue comes up after you and your client have signed a written contract).

❏ Develop an approach for handling toolkit, deliverables, and intellectual property rights issues in your client relationships. Then draft that approach into your template client contract.

❏ Intellectual property issues are complicated and trigger significant risks if not properly handled. Engage a lawyer with intellectual property experience to help you sort through these issues, define your objectives, and draft or review and revise contract language.

CHAPTER THREE - CONTRACTING WITH CLIENTS:

❏ Determine whether the proposed relationship with your client classifies you as an independent contractor or employee.

❏ Establish a process for on-boarding new clients that includes presenting them with and getting them to sign a written contract at the beginning of the relationship.

❏ Implement your on-boarding process, with reasonable flexibility.

❏ Research and engage a lawyer to help you determine the type of written contract to use.

❏ Research examples of other contracts to get familiar with what you might need in your contract.

❏ Engage a lawyer to help you create your template client contract.

❏ Use a written contract with each client.

❏ If your client presents you with its template contract, engage a lawyer to review it and help you negotiate reasonable changes.

❏ Use written subcontracts with your subcontractors that mirror or match the terms of the contract you have with your client for the project on which the subcontractor will work.

❏ Make sure all parties sign contracts and subcontracts correctly.

❏ Keep your signed contracts and subcontracts in a safe place for future reference if a question or dispute arises.

CHAPTER FOUR - CLIENT DISPUTES:

❏ Prepare for disputes before they occur

    ❏ Research your clients

    ❏ Draft provisions in your template client contract that provide an incentive to resolve disputes quickly.

    ❏ Create and use invoicing, payment, and collection practices that make it easier for your clients to pay.

❏ Remind clients when they haven't paid.

❏ If your client is unhappy with your services or deliverables, investigate the issue with them to determine the root cause, then review your contract to determine if you made any promises that your client believes you breached, and to identify potential remedies associated with a breach.

❏ If you can't deliver or deliver on time, communicate early, and often with your client. Consult your contract to determine how to proceed. If your contract is silent on this issue, negotiate a resolution with your client and make that resolution a written amendment to your contract.

❏ If your client wants a free fix, replacement, or refund, consult your contract to determine whether any of those remedies are available to it.

❏ If your client won't pay after exhausting your internal invoicing, payment, and collection procedures, engage a lawyer to send a demand letter, but only if you are prepared to sue if the client fails to pay after receiving the letter.

❏ If your client won't pay after your lawyer sends a demand letter, evaluate whether the economics justify filing a lawsuit to collect.

❏ File a lawsuit to collect, if economically justified.

❏ If your client sues you, check your state statutes to see if an LLC or corporation (whichever applies to your gig economy business) must be represented by a lawyer in court.

❑ If your client sues you, notify your insurer, if required, or engage a lawyer as soon as possible to defend your business so you don't suffer losses from failing to follow court rules and procedures when representing yourself.

CHAPTER FIVE - GETTING LEGAL HELP:

❑ Determine what legal services you need to start your gig economy business.

❑ Avoid incorporation services, document assembly services, and template stores because they do not offer legal advice.

❑ Conduct online research for a gig economy business lawyer. Supplement your internet research with recommendations from other professionals (e.g., CPA), colleagues, and competitors.

❑ Choose a few local lawyers and make an appointment for an initial consultation with each lawyer.

❑ Interview each lawyer you meet for potential fit based on her experience and personality.

❑ Ask each lawyer you meet to estimate the legal fees involved in forming your legal entity and drafting a template client contract.

❑ Engage the lawyer of your choice.

- ❏ If a client presents you with its contract or requested changes to your template client contract, ask your lawyer for an estimate of legal fees for review and revision.

- ❏ Engage your lawyer to review and revise contracts or requested changes from your client.

- ❏ Interact with your lawyer regularly as you work together on legal matters for your gig economy business.

Good luck!

Made in the
USA
Middletown, DE